WARRIOR

MAGNIFICENT

RADICAL RESULTS REQUIRE ZERO DOUBT

BY JAMIE VRINIOS

INDIGORIVER
PUBLISHING

WARRIOR
MAGNIFICENT

RADICAL RESULTS REQUIRE ZERO DOUBT

Editors: Donna Melillo, Kayte Middleton, Kim Rooks,
     Adam Tillinghast
Cover Design: Jason Kauffmann / Firelight Interactive /
     firelightinteractive.com
Cover Photo: Kimberly Dyer / kimberlydyerphotography.com
Interior Design: Kevin Williamson / kevinwilliamsondesign.com

Indigo River Publishing
3 West Garden Street Ste. 352
Pensacola, FL 32502
www.indigoriverpublishing.com

Ordering Information:
Quantity sales: Special discounts are available on quantity purchases by corporations, associations, and others. For details, contact the publisher at the address above.

Orders by U.S. trade bookstores and wholesalers: Please contact the publisher at the address above.

Printed in the United States of America

Publisher's Cataloging-in-Publication Data is available upon request.

Library of Congress Control Number: 2014934513

ISBN 978-0-9860493-8-5

First Edition

With Indigo River Publishing, you can always expect great books, strong voices, and meaningful messages. Most importantly, you'll always find ... words worth reading.

This book is dedicated to the Warrior Magnificent LOVES of my life: Peter, Nathan, Virginia, Amber, Samuel, Isaac, and Marilyn. You are a beautiful, endless reminder of God's unconditional LOVE, GRACE, and MAGNIFICENCE. Thank you for being the wind beneath my wings. I love you deeply and endlessly.

"The two most important days in your life are the day you are born and the day you find out why." - Mark Twain

CONTENTS

EMBRACE YOUR MAGNIFICENCE

Have you ever felt the pain of rejection? Let's be clear: I am referring to the in-your-face, you-are-nothing-to-me kind of rejection or abandonment. Can you remember who it was? Was it your friend, family member, classmate, or boyfriend? Maybe your peers or even your parents? Did that rejection have any kind of impact on your life? Do the opinions of others influence the pursuit of your dreams? Have you ever allowed rejection to make you question yourself and your MAGNIFICENCE? I can tell you this: overcoming rejection can be your greatest inspiration when you truly take ownership of your magnificence.

I consider myself an expert on rejection, especially the ultimate form of rejection—disownment. You see, my parents disowned me almost 30 years ago. Here's a quick synopsis: pregnant at 18, divorced, and disowned all within a three-year period of my life. My father, a much respected doctor, last laid eyes on me at the age of 19; and yes, I was labeled a "pregnant teenage" mom. However, that is just a small portion of my story. Before I tell you the rest, I want you to know that when I share my life experiences with you, it is straight from my HEART. My hope is that through my writing, you will feel compelled to pursue your magnificence.

You know, I didn't *have* to write this book. I *wanted* to write it because I really believe that even if one person can be inspired into their magnificence, then it is worth it. Why else would I expose my deepest hurts and pain to you? I believe passionately that the victory that emerged out of my pit moments is something that warriors will respond to and can rise up and do the same. This is not about me; it is about YOU—it is about anyone who truly wants to take ownership of their dream and break the limits society places on people.

Now back to my story ... Twenty-eight years ago, on April 14, 1985, I was in the delivery room experiencing the birth of my first baby boy. It was just hours after my grandmother had passed away miles from where I was living. My son Nathan was in my arms as the doctors assured me that my son and I were in perfect health. I remember that moment, looking into his beautiful eyes and feeling such an unconditional love for this precious miracle in my arms. A mother's instinctive gift to protect and nurture came easy for me, and the love I felt was overwhelming. Instantly, the pain of delivering this little miracle was replaced with the joy of being a mother.

This emotion was not new for me, as my daughter Amber was only 14 months old at the time. Giving birth to my children was an in-your-face reminder of the great MAGNIFICENCE we have all been created for—a gift freely given to us by our Creator. As I held my newborn son in my arms, the phone rang. It was my father on the other end. I hadn't seen or spoken to him in almost two years. He didn't stop to say, "How are you?" or "Congratulations!" Not that I expected him to. He simply made a statement: "Jamie, this is your father speaking. If you do not sign your rights over to the money your grandmother left you, then I will leave you nothing when I die." The conversation ended abruptly, and I was in complete shock.

Since that day, almost 30 years ago, I have not seen or spoken to my father, and my children are now 29, 28, and 16. Imagine the shock of not speaking to my father in two years and then hearing *those words* from him! It once again reminded me of the rejection I felt as a child. On that day, I experienced such great love and intense rejection all at the same time, in the very same moment. I was also faced with a stark choice that would impact my future and my children's future forever. I could feel sorry for myself and continue to believe that I was defective and had no value. I could buy into the label society had given to me: a "pregnant teenage mom" who was DISOWNED by her parents. Or, I could refuse to give rejection, abuse, and labels access to my life any longer and embrace the magnificence that I experienced every single time I looked at the gift of my children.

I can tell you that in that moment, looking at my beautiful children, I chose to stand up inside myself and summon the courage and the warrior within to live a life of MAGNIFI-CENCE. That phone call ignited something inside of me and caused me to embark on a fierce journey to never see my children or any other human being experience that kind of pain—the pain of *rejection*. As a single mom of two who was on public aid and completely disowned by my own parents and family, I made the decision to embrace my MAGNIFI-CENCE and rebuke the labels others imposed on me.

Looking back, I can tell you that there was absolutely no hesitation, no regret, and *no fear*. My purpose and passion to create something wonderful for my children was far greater than any challenge that I was experiencing or would experience in the future. Now, I honestly laugh in the face of rejection because it has only made me stronger.

By now you are probably wondering how a father and mother could disown their own daughter and grandchildren. This question flooded my mind frequently for several years after; however, there comes a time when every great leader must stop the recordings of the past and run toward the future, even if questions are still unanswered. After all, isn't that what faith is all about? Believing in what we can't see in the natural world while seeing a vivid picture in our minds? And after that phone call, with literally no family to support me—neither emotionally nor financially—I made a decision to take my life from the pit to the palace and design the life of my dreams ... to begin to believe in the vivid picture in my mind.

Can you imagine your ideal life? If you can imagine it, then you can create it—it's totally your choice! If you are really ready to get rid of your excuses, then this book might be for you. If you have a desire to maintain the same life or hang on to any form of a WIMPY MINDSET, it's best that you put this book down because you are not ready for the truth yet. If you are 99% into the pursuit of your dreams, then you will miss your goals *every single time*. Here's the TRUTH: half-committed leaders aren't ready to hear what it takes to develop a magnificent mindset. I can tell you this: it's *your choice, your life, your dreams.*

The questions we must ask ourselves now are these: Will we allow ourselves to let go of labels, status-quo thinking, and the fear of rejection? Will we step up and make an atypical move while we summon the warrior inside of us and create the life of our dreams?

I truly believe that when we make the choice to WIN, we encourage others to win. So ultimately, when we declare war on our demons, we inspire others to say farewell to theirs. We operate from a mindset that gives life and love to ourselves and the people around us, allowing our influence to become something of significance. We can contribute to others in a small way or even possibly help inspire them to take ownership of the birthright of their magnificence. The gift of encouragement we can offer to the world inspires greatness inside the very spirit of a person. It ignites the heart of the so-called rejects in the world—the very people like me who have been labeled, pushed aside, and rejected—to take a stand and walk in their magnificence.

We can inspire others to win—the children who are abused daily in unimaginable ways, the child bullied at school, the little boy who is teased because he isn't athletically inclined, the single mom people label as "dysfunctional," or better yet, the leader who takes a stand not to compromise their morals for the almighty dollar. The leaders who know they were born for greatness must take a stark stance and declare war on the labels society imposes on us all and that declares someone a "winner" or a "loser" based on how well they fit inside a mold. Summoning the courage to win by going against the status quo of average thinking inspires us to take ownership of our magnificence.

I have walked through this fierce journey of rejection, and I no longer focus on the past. Since the day I chose to fight for my magnificence, my dreams, and my future, I continue to propose the same question to myself: "Jamie, *dream* or *die*? It's totally up to you." I can tell you exactly what I choose to live my life by, and that is dream—absolutely DREAM!

Dream as BIG as you can, and be as MAGNIFICENT as you see yourself. This is *your life, your choice, your magnificence!* We have the ability to create whatever we want by the very thoughts we think on a daily basis. So let me ask you this question: why did you pick up this book? What are you searching for? Many people will pick up this book; however, only true warriors will have the courage to pursue their magnificence. You may think you are a warrior, but have you ever *really* taken a FIERCE stance on something you believe in? I am not referring to mentally disagreeing with something. I am talking about a really fierce, *unwavering* stance that literally means life or death to who you are and why you were created. Do the challenges in life impact your decision to pursue your magnificence? If they do, you are not a warrior yet—and you may not be able to handle this book. Are you waiting for the people around you to agree with where you are going? If you are seeking public approval, then you are not a warrior yet, and this book may not be for you.

You may wonder how I have the GUTS to say this. If you really read the first few paragraphs of my story, then you would know deep down that when you have overcome the obstacles I have—gone from nothing to building a multimillion dollar organization—then you can call yourself an expert on what is required to develop a warrior mindset. Do the challenges of life overwhelm you, toss you back and forth, leave you doubting and putting your dreams on HOLD, or even make you forget them? If that is you, then you most *definitely* should finish this book. You either need to find your dreams again or put this book down—because you may not be ready for the truth of what it takes to create a life of magnificence. Seriously, I want to capture the hearts and minds of warriors with this book. I want you all to become leaders who embrace the truth and are really ready to have the fearless conversations required for *real* transformation.

Have you been rejected? Or maybe even labeled as a "dreamer," "different," "loser," "unworthy," "misfit," "a disgrace," "crazy," "disowned," "nerd," or "misunderstood"? Well, I can tell you this much: I get it! If you have the GUTS to finish this book and take a *fierce stance* today—to let go of all the insults, labels, scars, challenges, and pain from your past and WIN—then consider yourself a warrior! It's time to take these great lessons from your life and draw strength rather than allowing these memories to weaken you and prevent you from creating anything of significance. It's your choice now: *Dream and live,* or *doubt and die.* You see, holding on to the past will only feed into a pitiful mindset. Letting go inspires a powerful mindset, bringing manifestation of the MAGNIF-ICENT into your present and future. Ok ... so before I finish my story, you must make a choice ... do you choose PITIFUL or POWERFUL? WIMP or WARRIOR? Remember ... *your life, your choice, your dream.* Change your mindset—change your life *forever.* From the pit to the palace—this is *your* Cinderella story, so you are faced with a stark choice.

VISION

THE COLORFUL PAINTING
IN YOUR MIND

Just a ye   und
m   er the
age o   d
ever be   . I
will nev   ife
because   I
wasn't va   n-
ships with   g
to observe t   d
just walk aw   n
to honor theiand I guess I n   ed to marry
David when I f   pregnant. In fact, the wedding
occurred just 24 hours after I told my parents I was pregnant,
and that was the last day I laid eyes on my dad—almost 30
years ago. We got married fast so we could get back to school.
Not once did anyone give this teenage mom any kind of
counseling. That was just the way it was going to be. I adapted
to this mindset because that was exactly how my mind was
trained; I just had to accept it.

You see, we believe what we have convinced our mind to believe. Until we create new thoughts, we will never see new behaviors—or new beginnings to the life we dream of living. Our lives are portraits of what we have accepted or rejected as our own truths—whether this was imposed on us as children or discovered as students searching to find our own answers along the way. As a child, my truth was: "You do what you are told—without question—or you will get knocked around." So, that is what I believed at the time I got pregnant.

Looking back, I now know that fear was being instilled in my daily life. Projecting fear into human beings does not inspire them to be great. Fear is the opposite of faith, and this assault weapon of fear is most definitely in pursuit to cut off any seed of MAGNIFICENCE if we allow it to take root. I ask myself this all the time: Why would we allow anyone to speak anything but greatness into our lives? After all, we have the *power* to WALK AWAY! If you are in a situation that leaves you feeling helpless, powerless, unmotivated, or doubtful, my advice to you is to RUN. My marriage was unhealthy from the beginning—but what should you expect when you allow other people to dictate or decide who you will marry with absolutely no sound advice in moving toward your DREAMS? It was just the way it was going to be.

As a little girl, I remember being told that children are to be seen and not heard. I was living out the very things that were spoken to me as a child, and I had accepted this picture of myself. But deep down, I knew that something was terribly wrong. Remember, I am a warrior, and all warriors know when something is not quite right—but will all warriors have the courage to act? We know that when we have unhealthy relationships in our lives, the stop signs often pop up. But we slowly start to convince ourselves that maybe it's not really that bad.

Maybe what's wrong isn't an actual relationship with another person. Maybe it's the partnership we've been having with our dream—our MAGNIFICENCE. It could be limits we place on our dream. When we place limits on our dream, we find ourselves accepting less than what we desire for our lives because it got tough along the way.

Maybe you slowly allowed status-quo, fearful, negative thinking to take root. Is this what you *really* want for your life? Take a snapshot of the people you are being influenced by. Do they make statements like "It's not so bad"? Or maybe they continually remind you that there are people who have it *way* worse than you. Didn't you know that you're lucky? That you should just appreciate what you have and accept the average like everyone else? The question isn't about who has it worse or better than you. The real truth we must ask ourselves is *"What about me?"* What about that deep-down feeling that keeps summoning you to get up and fight for something bigger than average? Consider this: *Dream and live* or *doubt and die?* The warrior may seem to be temporarily confused at times when pressure kicks in; but deep down, warriors can see and feel *clarity* because they know one thing: YES, I am born for something way beyond average. I am destined for MAGNIFICENCE!

I find it so contradictory that we can teach our little girls and boys to dream, but we can't dream ourselves. We encourage our children by reading fairy tales—maybe we even visit Disney World and speak dreams into them with unwavering belief and enthusiasm that they can be *anything* they dream to be—yet we stop feeding our own minds with this same truth. I mean seriously, how many books have you read your children on dreaming? I know that I love fairy tales. I love happy movies with beautiful endings, and I choose to still watch and embrace the child-like message of faith from these books and movies because it keeps me DREAMING.

I love going to Disney World and dreaming, and I am always inspired by the little girls dancing around Cinderella's castle dressed up as beautiful princesses. You can just feel the joy exuding from them the second they walk out of the Bibbidi Bobbidi Boutique. I see these little girls take one look at Cinderella, and BAM! Their hearts are smiling so bright! The reason everyone lights up is that Cinderella WON by dreaming of a better life! Cinderella inspires the princess warrior in us, and we want to win just like she did.

Have you ever asked yourself why anyone would ever stop dressing up like a prince or a princess? The world looks at queens, kings, presidents, and those in Hollywood in awe. Why not look at *yourself* with the same pair of eyes and believe?

> *"Write the vision And make it plain on tablets,*
> *That he may run who reads it. For the vision*
> *is yet for an appointed time; But at the end it*
> *will speak, and it will not lie. Though it tarries,*
> *wait for it; Because it will surely come, It will*
> *not tarry."*
> – Habakkuk 2:2-3

God has created you for MAGNIFICENCE, so stop looking around you and start seeing YOU! The only difference between you and the people you admire is the *pure belief* in who you are and your UNIQUE MAGNIFICENCE. The slipper fits your foot perfectly, so place it on your foot and start walking in your destiny now, not later.

The words and pictures that we paint in our mind display a self-portrait of someone who is either powerful or pitiful. We have a choice to see ourselves living in a pit or a palace by the thoughts we think and the words we speak. What kind of words are you wrapping around yourself and your dreams? When was the last time you picked up a fairy tale book or watched a movie that actually encouraged the childlike spirit in you? Let me remind you that right now you are reading one of those so-called "fairy tale" books—and guess what? Dreams *do* come true! Remember me—the teenage pregnant mom who was disowned and labeled "unworthy" almost 30 years ago? Just like Cinderella, nothing could change the picture in my mind. I knew deep down that I was born to be a PRINCESS. When you know you are a princess, it doesn't matter what happens in your life, simply because NOBODY has the power to remove or paint a permanent picture on you without your permission. Stop giving other people or yourself permission to paint anything less but magnificence in your mind and heart.

I absolutely love to speak to little ones because there is unquestionably nothing but pure LOVE and BELIEF pouring out of them so effortlessly. Their imagination and dreams are LIMITLESS! All of us have the ability to dream like a little child, but we must get rid of the old paintings and embrace the new. The things that have hurt you and held you back—whatever it is or was—*let it go!* In my own life, I had to be *intentional* about having a funeral with my past. And now, my life is *exactly* the way I painted it to be—and by the way, I am not finished with my fairy tale ending. Here's a truth: *Your life is* exactly *what you have imagined and spoken it to be.* You wouldn't believe the things that I convinced my mind into believing ... things that drew me into one unhealthy situation after another. The most important thing we can ever do in life is keep moving forward and stop looking back. That is exactly what I did. My marriage ended, and the warrior in me continued to move forward with a fearless mindset to *dream and live* or *doubt and die.*

PARASITE OR PROTÉGÉ?

Today as I was walking on the beach, I was reminded once again of how grateful I am to have developed a sound warrior mindset—a mindset that is not willing to waiver in the midst of adversity. I believe that this mindset has continually served me well in the choice I am faced with daily: *Dream and live* or *doubt and die*. I learned so much during my two-year journey as my body was attacked by a parasite. I remember looking at myself in the mirror—5 feet 8½ inches tall, weighing just 95 pounds. I may have resembled a skeleton on the outside, but I was still a WARRIOR on the inside. I can tell you that the WARRIOR in me was determined to win. Even though almost everyone who saw me didn't believe I would make it without "traditional" thinking, I knew deep down inside me that I would win! God placed the courage in me that if I could see myself healed, then I would be.

I remember that the invasion of parasites felt so similar to the invasion I felt when rejection tried to attack my mind, spirit, and body at the age of 19. I was ready to battle this thing because I chose to focus on the *healer*, not my *symptoms*. I believe that in all of us, God has put the spirit of courage, not fear—the ability to rise up and conquer *anything* that launches an attack on our destiny. I had gone through six months of testing, antibiotics, and opinions, but still the weight was falling off daily. My physical body was getting weaker; however, my MIND and my SPIRIT were transforming into something beyond what my human mind could comprehend. I was feeling a supernatural power that could only be explained by a power much bigger than me. I was meditating daily on scriptures that I could wrap my mind and spirit around that resonated with me and encouraged me to WIN. The warrior continued to rise up inside of me. I could see myself 100% healthy, and that was my first step.

In fact, this is the first step for all warriors in realizing their dreams—we must SEE it first. Dreamers who can *see it* will convince their mind to *know it*, and that will summon the courage to *speak it*. Eventually, they will live out what they see and speak. The truth, if you can handle it, is this: we are our own prophet, so everything we have in our life, we have brought into manifestation by the very *thoughts* that we have believed in enough to speak and convinced our spirits to act on. Then BAM! We have what we say.

I was getting no sound advice from the doctors, yet I knew that I was going to get through it and be healed. I believe in a God who HEALS, and I found myself having to completely ignore the medical community—as well as the majority of people and their opinions—and focus on what I *saw* and what I *knew*. I have learned that we have to ignore the symptoms of disease. We have to step away from the logical, traditional status quo and believe in what we *know* with 100% faith.

Personally, I decided not to share my so-called "illness" with the multitudes because I knew they didn't have the faith to believe what I already KNEW. I *am healed*. How many people are you sharing your dream with, but deep inside, you know they don't get it? *Stop sharing it with them.* When you get to the finish line, then share your victory! You don't need their advice because they are not a dreamer who really believes or else they would get it. For me, there was a handful of people who really KNEW what was happening—and within that circle, only two had the fierce faith to really stand with me in my healing.

If we can see ourselves whole, complete, healed, and living our dreams out loud, God will provide the answers. How many times do we focus on our symptoms instead of creating the mindset that is required to see ourselves living out our dreams? When we allow our dreams to be put on hold, the heart grows weary. Depression is potential screaming to come out of you.

Can I ask you a question? What is your "THIS"? I'm sure you are probably wondering what I am referring to. Your "THIS" is that deep-down feeling—the true desire of your heart—that keeps surfacing in your mind saying, "HELLO? Did you forget me?" Your "THIS" will never go away because "THIS" is what you are created to live out. "THIS" is a permanent fixture—one of those things you can't remove from who you are no matter what. You may try to ignore it, but you can't because it is your unique gift and the very reason you were born. It is the part that nobody really understands except you and our Creator because He put it there. It is the very essence of *everything* you represent. Anything that you have ever envisioned in your mind for your life is all in your "THIS."

If you will pursue your dreams with *total passion*. "THIS" is impossible to lose. Pursuing your MAGNIFICENCE inspires your "THIS"—an essence inside every single one of us.

Tell me why you are here on earth—to pay your bills? To wake up every single day and do the same thing over and over like a little hamster in a cage? I look around at so many people living just like a little hamster—going around and around on an endless journey to nowhere. I have also observed very gifted warriors accepting the status-quo mentality because they gave in to fear, doubted their symptoms of dis-ease, and decided to live a life with limits, sedating the very "THIS" they are born with.

It is your *birthright* to live a limitless life, so why accept anything less? I can tell you that almost everyone but a handful of people were imposing limits on my so-called diagnosis—not just at that point in my journey, but all throughout my life. They were feeding into a parasitic and toxic mindset, not a warrior mentality. If we are honest with ourselves, anyone who has ever truly pursued their dreams will encounter the small-minded people in the world who tell us to give up. They will encourage defeat before they will believe and expect victory.

I can tell you that it was my faith that kept me alive—not a pill or an opinion. The same goes for your dreams. It will not be opinions that keep your destiny alive; it will be *you* and your faith in your God-given MAGNIFENCE.

Please hear me: *Nobody can do this but YOU!* If you don't act on your dreams and come against any form of invasion into your mind, body, soul, and spirit, then your destiny, your dreams, and the very reason you are here will die. We actually have total control over the limits we impose on ourselves. All warriors understand this.

Unfortunately, I had no control over my bowels, and it was if I were in a body of a 150 year-old. I was totally and completely humbled by the realization that I had no control over my body; however, I did have the power to control my thoughts daily. The mindset I continually created for myself was focusing on being 100% healthy and never allowing the symptoms of the dis-ease to gain any kind of strength or momentum. How many times as leaders have we faced adversity, challenges, or obstacles—whatever we want to name it—and people have obsessed about the problem, the symptom, when none of those thoughts bring power to the very truth of what we desire to live out our dreams. I knew deep inside that I would be healed, even when I looked like a skeleton. When it was getting really scary, I remember Peter and others saying, "Jamie, are you sure you shouldn't LISTEN to the doctors? After all, they know what they are doing." But you have to understand that when you really believe what you know, you don't hesitate in following what you know. This is when you see results.

I had zero doubt that God would provide the answers and the healing because He wouldn't give me the vision or strength to stand alone unless He was planning on keeping His promise. Every dreamer is given a vision. If you are given a vision, I can guarantee that you have the gifts—your "THIS"—already inside you to see it come to full manifestation. I describe it like this: If you were to look at a package of seeds for roses, you would see a picture of a beautiful rose garden on the package.

Somehow, your mind is convinced that if you plant the seed in the ground, you will grow a beautiful garden. So you plant the seed, and you believe in time you will get what you planted. A few weeks go by, then BAM! You have a rose garden! Let me ask you this: Did you scream at the seed? Did you doubt the seed? Or did you just see it? Know it enough to take action, plant it, and watch your garden manifest.

Dreamers have to understand that if we want to see our seed come into full manifestation, then we must believe that the seed is the dream God has placed inside us. We must also understand that the fruit in our life is not for us—it is for others. Does the apple tree bear fruit for the apple tree? Or does it bear fruit to bring life and nourishment to every living creature that eats the fruit from this tree? I can tell you that it is absolutely no different with *your dream*, *your destiny*, *your purpose*.

Sometimes the situation seemed discouraging; but isn't this the same when the storms come and hit the very seeds we plant in a garden? We can't control the storms in life, but we can control our thoughts and actions on how we apply what we know deep down in our guts.

Do not *ever, ever, ever* let anyone anywhere make you question your gut. That is a *God-given gift*. The logical, so-called "proven" textbook mindset is a JOKE. It is there for those people who are too afraid to dream, act, and believe in the *miraculous*. I'm not sure about you, but I am so ready to stand with warriors who actually believe that if God gives us the ability to *see it*, then HECK YES we can *have it* when we take a fierce stance in what we see. I can tell you after six months, then eight months, and almost one year of dealing with my dis-ease, I was completely done with the logical and ready to embrace the miraculous.

If we want to see actual change—transformation in our lives—there comes a time that we actually deal with the root of this dis-ease. For me, it was refusing to believe anything other than what I knew deep inside me. I am now 100% healed and healthy. I can tell you that the words I have lived my life by helped me here: "*You are created for something MAGNIFICENT!*" I refused to accept anything but what I saw, and that is something marvelous. Like I said, the only dis-ease that we have in our lives is what we allow our minds to believe. If you see yourself magnificent, you will become what you see. You are MAGNIFICENT, and don't EVER · allow anything make you doubt it!

Believing in my magnificence , gave me the power, confidence, and courage to go against the logical, boring, uneventful, majority-rules opinions. You may be saying, "Wow, Jamie, you were really taking a risk!" I guess you're right about that, if I were entertaining doubt. But the truth is that I had ZERO DOUBT. If you want *radical* results in your life, you must have zero doubt. Only the mindset of a warrior can even grasp what I am saying because most people entertain doubt on a consistent basis. They have allowed this parasite to become a permanent part of their daily thoughts, but the parasite of doubt will only take them in the opposite direction of their dreams. The people you love the most may not get it, and they don't have to. This is *your life,* remember? The lesson, journey, or so-called "experience" is YOURS.

The symptoms you experience disappear when you create a mindset that declares WAR on the parasites that will try to invade *your* dream.

You may never literally contract a parasite like I did; however, you must agree that if you are not pursuing your dreams with PASSION and VIGOR, then you have allowed parasites to infest your mind and delay your dreams. Are you focused on the opinion of the "experts" who are advising solutions that go against your gut and your "THIS"? Maybe their advice seems to make sense, but that does not make it *true* for your life and your dreams, does it?

DILIGENCE

For months, Peter and I took long walks on the beach, praying for and believing in the miraculous. This wasn't something we did every now and then—it was daily and diligently. We collected hundreds of sand dollars as we walked and spoke about my healing—the breakthrough and the moment when it would all come together and I would finish victoriously. I never missed a day speaking and believing what I could see vividly in my mind. Warriors are not negotiating for anything less than the finish they see from the beginning of the race.

If you can see it, you can have it when you are willing to take action diligently. Breakthrough is your permission slip to move to a new level in reaching your dreams. The greatest resistance will come when a breakthrough is about to occur; and you must be diligent in this pursuit, or you will fall short every single time. The character of a leader is revealed under pressure, and the words that come out of our mouths during the squeezing process reveal a portrait of what is *really* going on in our minds. In my 20 years of encouraging entrepreneurs and leaders, I have been shocked to see what happens to someone who chooses to maintain anything less than a warrior mindset during a battle for their dreams. It is quite frankly really sad when the leader is playing to lose because they have no chance of any great victory. The mindset created by this kind of thinking is average—and we can agree that average has never helped anyone embrace magnificence. *Average is the best of the worst and the worst of the best.*

Playing to lose is like someone telling you that it is okay to just exist but not live. When the mirror reflected back to me when I was a 95-pound skeletal version of myself, I could have gathered the majority around me who play to lose, and they would have given me permission to QUIT. They would have felt sorry for me. However, when warriors are fighting battles, we are not looking for someone to feel pity for us. On the contrary, warriors are praying for other warriors who are stronger than themselves to enter into their lives. These warriors have experience in winning great battles and can actually lend wisdom and strength to us so that we can summon the courage to WIN. Remember, warriors have no desire to enlist wimps on their team because they are definitely going into *every* battle knowing that the victory is already won.

Surround yourself with warriors or hang out with the wimps who have made the word QUIT a permanent fixture in their minds. When you find yourself surrounded by the wimps of the world, my advice from one warrior to another is RUN! It's your choice, your mindset, your life to live. *Dream and live* or *doubt and die.*

The ongoing status-quo stance will never prove to be a powerful choice in your breakthrough, so set your mind on attracting the warriors. How many wimpy, small-minded people are giving you advice about your dream? The longer we entertain the very thought of defeat, the more time we give it to take root. Instead of the beautiful picture we saw in our mind—remember the beautiful rose garden (our dreams, our MAGNIFICENCE)—well, it will be soon replaced with weeds choking the very life out of anything new that we create and that will lead us to our dreams. I remember when I met my holistic warriors who helped me WIN my parasite battle. One of the warriors said to me, "Jamie, your body will go through a healing crisis, so don't be shocked if you get worse before you get better."

I asked myself, "What the heck?! How could it get *worse?*" However, I knew deep down that he was right. If I was serious about my healing, then I had to embrace the truth of what he said and change my mindset once again. My mindset was, *"Okay. Let's win this battle! Tell me what to do, and I will do it."*

Pursuing a dream and having *real confidence* in your MAGNIFICENCE just sounds like too much. After all, it is only for a few very special people in the world, right? Absolutely NOT the truth! We slowly adjust ourselves to a parasitic invasion, not even aware that we have started to compromise our mindset just so we can appease and allow dis-ease to become permanent. We don't even realize what has happened because we are being killed slowly.

Then all of a sudden, you pick up a book where the author is actually telling you the RAW truth of what it takes to create a successful life and walk in your God-given gifts—your actual BIRTHRIGHT—and BAM! Your first instinct might be to reject it because it doesn't come wrapped in the pretty package you have been familiar with, but still, you start reading. The warrior inside is longing to keep reading because the truth is something a warrior is hungry for. A warrior wants to hear the raw truth of what it takes to actually win a freaking battle! We all love to hear the story of a great comeback, right? But you also have to face things like your daily habits and how you contracted this parasite mindset.

We are now starting the healing crisis—the point that things get worse before they get better. A leader who has a mindset of refusing to go through the healing crisis to get rid of the dis-ease in their life will start to convince the mind to accept excuses, blame games, and the average and will eventually go along with status-quo thinking again. When you want to be cured, don't you have to remove the things that are causing your dis-ease from your diet? YES! Absolutely so!

My *entire* lifestyle changed. I was already eating healthy, but then I REALLY had some stark choices to make because I was going to a whole new level of eating and living. Warriors understand that our daily habits will infuse life or death into our dreams. Leaders will have to ask themselves, *"What kind of diet have I allowed which has created this parasitic invasion in the first place?"* If you truly want to get better, you must welcome the truth and make immediate changes to win the battle. If you have any form of dis-ease and you don't make the right changes in your diet and life, the parasites will spread, and you will DIE. Remember: *your choice, your mindset, your life.*

The first step is deciding to trust yourself and the mentors that have been placed in your life for this break-through. Without trust, we can never see full manifestation of our MAGNIFICENCE.

Now take a quick snapshot of the mentors in your life. Are they warriors or wimps? Do they have any warrior qualities in them at all to assist you in this battle of a lifetime? I know that the mentors in my life *definitely* play to win! Do yours? If they don't, well, how do you expect any REAL transformation? I believe my success in every area of my life can be directly connected to my mentors. For me, one of the greatest loves of my life is my mentor for 20-plus years, Marilyn Welle. I will never forget when she was placed in my life when I was 27. For the first time EVER, I just *knew* that she had the key to my very destiny. It was that deep, deep feeling again. I just *knew* she was put in my life for a divine reason, to help me move to a new level.

This is the exact same feeling you will have when any great warrior enters your life. Here I was—a single mom of two—and she shows up and teaches me about ME! She helped me confront all the parasites in my life, including the family members who cast me aside like a defective piece of machinery. I will never forget the day she spoke to me for the first time over the phone. It was like she just *knew* my magnificence. I had the exact same feeling when I met my holistic warriors. They knew how to help me. You see, all warrior encounters will bring you to a new level at different times of your life.

Maybe you picked this book up because you are really at dis-ease in your life and ready to see real transformation. You are excited to find advice that can really help you; however, suddenly you realize that if want to see real change and growth to get free of dis-ease and walk in magnificence, you have to be willing to make some tough choices. At first it seems everything is going great, but then life happens. It might be the people around you who don't get it or don't support you. Maybe your finances are being squeezed because you are investing financially in your dream. It could even be a physical symptom of pain. Whatever it may be, these parasites start to tell you why you can't do it, and they give you all the "logical" reasons why it will fail. Hey—I get it, people! Seriously. My whole *life* has been a training ground for my mind, and I am *clear* as to what you must do. Maybe you decided that since things aren't happening fast or instantly, it is a sign from God that your dream is not meant to be. (Which, by the way, is a *total cop-out and part of a wimpy mindset.*)

How many times are we are so close to embarking on the NEW, but then our enthusiasm turns to doubt. Once again, we allowed the "parasites" to invade our mind and confirm our doubt instead of inspiring HOPE and bringing out the very best in us. We have to speak to the warrior in us, not the wimp. I see the parasite of doubt invade the mind of leaders that I mentor daily. And you know what? Eventually doubt wins if they choose to entertain it for very long. I have seen so many great leaders cave under pressure when the healing crisis starts, and they find themselves leaving their dream behind because the "side effects" were more painful to them than the PASSION to pursue their BEST. The dream doesn't go away, however, because your MAGNIFICENCE—the "seed" that you were born with—will never disappear. In fact, it is impossible to completely ignore it. You feel it calling you in the quiet times of your mind, and you find yourself looking back with regret. You're tormented about the decision to quit and surrounding yourself with the other wimps who also made the choice to give up.

I truly believe that we are who we surround ourselves with. When you decide to wimp out, the only people around you are other quitters. It would *have* to be other wimps because warriors won't hang around quitters. Keep in mind if you are a warrior or you are with a warrior, something inside you will rise up, encouraging others to get back up and FIGHT for their dreams. The crowd that believes in mediocrity agrees with the mindset of giving up because it helps justify their inaction. But the truth is this: They just didn't have the GUTS to summon the warrior.

Like I've said before, there are two kinds of people in the world: warriors and wimps. Warriors are passionate about where they are going and are most definitely not interested in what the majority may think. They are consumed with living out their magnificence and inspiring others to do the same. The warrior gives energy. There is a presence that exudes from them—a confidence and a countenance that they *know* they are destined for something MAGNIFICENT.

Warriors have a PASSION to battle for others. They lead the battle to inspire, encourage, and stand up no matter what other leaders say while inspiring those leaders to find their best version possible. They don't complain about their problems because they understand that everyone had life happen to them. You never know when a warrior is really struggling because they are too focused on other people. This is what gives them this supernatural energy. When we focus on people and love, somehow our problems seem to go away. We must always remember deep down that *we are here to be a blessing to others, not just to ourselves.*

When a warrior walks in the room, everyone is drawn to this energy because it is *strong* and *unwavering* and *fearless.* People can FEEL the warrior in you; and believe me, when all heck breaks loose in someone's life, don't think for a moment they want a wimp. The humans on this earth who are in any kind of battle want a warrior because they want someone who has a contagious fearlessness and refuses to quit at the first sign of adversity. Warriors don't go into battle and run away at the first sign of adversity.

Warriors love the challenge and are not looking for an easy way out. They want to know that when they get to the other side, they are stronger and wiser, so they can help other warriors cross. If you ask a warrior how they are doing, no matter how they may feel, you can bet they will say "GREAT!" because every day, they are speaking and living what they see in their mind ... MAGNIFICENCE!

If you ask a wimp (or we can call them an energy parasite), they will tell you all the horrible things that have happened to them. When you leave their presence, you feel like a pile of leeches have literally sucked the blood right out of you. The wimps are constantly telling you what they hate about their job, their husband, their dog—you name it, they say it! And you know what? The truth is that they are revealing just how self-absorbed they are. Negative people are just self-absorbed; it's all about them and never about others.

I know you have met these special individuals. In fact, maybe *you* are an energy parasite, and it is time to make a change in your attitude! Focus on something other than YOU. The TRUTH—if we can all handle it—is that the very things people complain about, they have the power to change or they wouldn't be complaining! If you don't like your husband, why are you married to him? If you don't like your dog, for God's sake, give that sweet dog to someone who loves animals! But please just SHUT UP and go be MAGNIFICENT! The reason people are tired all the time is that they hang around tired, wimpy people, not warriors! You don't see warriors sitting around waiting on something to be dropped in their lap. They are in BATTLE because they know that's when they feel the most powerful. They are fighting for someone or something somewhere, and that ignites their HEART.

Ladies and Gentlemen, when we are focused on others, we are inspired because our fruit is not for ourselves. It is for others. Do you know how much MAGNIFICENCE is inside of you right now, screaming to come out? I am continually amazed and actually perplexed by the obsession this world has with watching other people live their lives on television. What the heck are you doing?! What about *your* life? You have a destiny to pursue! Who freaking cares what the desperate housewives are doing? And that is just one example! It's a message that we have nothing better to do than gossip, fight, and be self-absorbed.

I remember walking out in the ocean waist deep and searching for sand dollars, knowing that they were a rare find, but believing that God would bring them to me if I continued to search and believe. I know that many of you will find that hard to understand, but I was literally training my mind and speaking things out while expecting it to show up because I was 100% sure that a miracle was going to occur. I was working on my warrior mindset, the mindset of *"I refuse to lose."*

After months of dealing with this dis-ease, I was getting ready to walk on the beach and collect sand dollars when it happened. I looked outside. It was cloudy and had been raining on and off, but I wanted to go take my walk. Peter had something to do with our son, so I decided to drive to the beach. As I got to the beach, the rain was slightly drizzling, and I could see a rainbow in the sky between some dark clouds. At that moment, I looked at the rainbow, smiled, and said, "That's right. I am healed."

Because of the weather, the beach was empty. I started to take my walk and was just smiling inside because I could feel something really amazing happening. It was faith and hope rising up inside me. Many of you may find this a common experience; but for me, this was different than what I experienced on any of my walks before. This was something more extraordinary. I felt like something was there. I had been waiting for this moment for a very long time, and now I felt like I was actually in it for real.

As I was walking back to my car, there was an elderly man in the water by himself. I found this odd because of the bad weather. I thought to myself, *"Who would be in the water on a rainy day like this, especially an elderly man?"* As I walked past him, he asked me this question: "Do you have far to go?"

With a smile, I replied, "No."

He said, "You know, young lady, when the rain comes, it comes fast."

My smile grew, I said, "Yes. That is true."

In that moment, what he said to me was a message I interpreted as this: "When He shows up for the miracle you have been praying for, it will happen suddenly. And you will be overwhelmed with JOY!"

I was running and smiling and just believing, I was thinking, "WOW! *Thank you God for the WINK!*" In my heart of hearts, the question that was proposed to me was, "Jamie, when you are healed, then what?"

My answer was simple: "I want to bless the children of this world, not just by feeding them or clothing them. I want to feed them God's love and clothe them in the MAGNIFICENCE that they are created for!" In that moment, my desire went far beyond my own needs or even my healing. It was focused on what would I do if I were ever given a platform to make a difference, and the answer was LOVE. I was so sure in that moment that my life would be changing dramatically.

So many times I see leaders give up under pressure. If they would have just pushed through, they would have seen their dream manifested. The birthing process is painful; however, it is necessary. And any great leader understands that pressure applied only makes us stronger when we push through. I think we would all agree that you can't be a "little pregnant." When you are pregnant, it is obvious to those around you, and you are in it for the long-haul. The same should be applied to our dreams. When you are about to breakthrough to your dreams, the moment you stand in what you were born for, you look back and realize it was ALL WORTH IT.

If you can *see it*, you can *be it*! So, I dare you to step into your boldness and not back down on what you know. You will never be the same. I promise. I learned to train my mind, thoughts, and actions from pitiful to powerful starting at a very young age. If I had fed the pitiful-and-disowned-doctor's-daughter mindset, my life and my kids' lives would be a whole different story, now wouldn't it? If I looked at my body as pitiful and unhealthy instead of vibrant and healthy, this book would not be in your hands. A lesson well-learned in my life: never apologize for your power, and never let anyone try to take it from you. This is your choice—no one else's. Warriors never operate from a PITIFUL mindset. They have created and exude a mindset beyond POWERFUL.

IMAGINE

*It is in our decisions we make daily that
our destiny is shaped. This is totally up
to you and only you ... where do you
IMAGINE yourself to be?*

When my family and I go to Disney World, I love the rollercoasters. In one of the theme parks, one roller-coaster takes you from 0 to 65mph in just 2.8 seconds. Can you imagine taking your life from the pit to the palace this fast? When warriors put their minds in an acceleration mode, they can indeed arrive at their destination in record time. If you can *see it*, then you can *have it*, as long as you are willing to take daily action on what you see in your mind. You can live a life of limitless possibilities. We have the life we do because we first imagined it, and you will have what you imagine your life to be. Imagining is dreaming. So, what is your dream, and how big can you dream, baby? Imagining is the first step in manifesting the invisible into your reality.

Success is a decision in the mind FIRST. You will create your destiny by what you see, believe, and speak and by what you are determined enough to take action on. A warrior in pursuit of magnificence requires the DNA of a *faith giant*.

You must see yourself living out your dreams FIRST, and this requires you to *speak daily into your life everything you imagine it to be.* We shall have what we *see* and what we *speak* it to be, because our words hold power—so watch your mouth! Your action toward what you see in your mind is confirmation that you really have the faith to bring your dreams into the magnificent.

When was the last time you imagined yourself to be off-the-charts successful? It's time for you to become totally confident in your future—walking in faith, not fear, and embracing the vision that God has placed in your heart. It's time for you to see yourself prosperous in every area of your life. Warriors are faith giants and go into battle to win, not lose. This requires that they be addicted to faith and the commitment it takes to manifest the magnificent. They strive to complete their assignment in life. Warriors speak up and speak out because they aim to win, not lose. This requires they know it well, and yes, they EXPECT it.

Are you ready to experience the ride of your life? Imagine living a life of limitless possibilities. You are! *It's totally* up to you to. Remember: *dream and live* or *doubt and die. Your choice. Your life. Your dream.* Limitless is defined as unrestricted without limits, boundless in amount, infinite, endless, never ending, vast, countless immeasurable, numberless, unlimited, and untold. It is infinity and beyond! Are you ready for this kind of MAGNIFICENCE? Do you know that we are born to think limitless? Our imagination is vivid as a child; but as the years go by, it can become suppressed by the negative, limited words spoken over our life.

I remember when my life went from 0 to 65 in 2.8 seconds, and I believe it happened because I imagined it to be FIRST. As a single mom going from corporate America to starting my own business, my imagination served me well. In fact, it has served me well my entire life. Everyone told me how secure my corporate America job was, but I soon found myself jobless because I would not compromise my standards for a promotion.

One day, I was brought into a boardroom. The owner told me that the company was restructuring and would no longer need me. The warrior inside me rose up again, and I said to myself, *"I already know the ending to this story of Cinderella. And guess what? I WIN!"* So instead of attacking the two men who fired me for no real reason, I chose to let it go and move on to the next chapter of my life. After all, who has time to dwell on the negative and on the past when the future is waiting for no one and time isn't going to slow down?

So many people spend their lives thinking about the past when their future is so much brighter. Warriors know they are always required to let go in order to move forward because no baggage is welcome. I truly believe that everything happens for a reason and that there are no coincidences in life. No one is ever prepared for these shocks in life, but they don't matter because these shocks are the training ground where we develop warrior strength that brings the magnificent into our lives and those around us.

At that time, I had no one I could depend on—no one I could even borrow a dime from. You know what I have realized? Some of the most beautiful blessings are wrapped in

the craziest packages, and they don't have a big bright bow
on them. They actually require discipline, persistence, and
WORK. If you want to see your life go from 0 to 65 in 2.8
seconds, then you must be ready for the ride and ready to
work hard. Magnificence is not free. Remember that there is
a price tag, and there are ZERO discounts. After being let go,
I decided to become the CEO, CFO, and owner of my own
business. It's funny how so many people laughed at my choice
to pursue this opportunity, but a warrior doesn't enlist public
opinion. Warriors follow their guts with fierce faith. I took this
opportunity and ran with it, only to find myself moving at an
accelerated rate—from 0 to 65 in 2.8 seconds. Soon, I found
myself making more money than I had ever made in corporate
America, and I discovered that everything in my imagination
was now connected to another source. This would assist me in
making my dreams come true.

There were many obstacles along the way; but for me,
they were only confirmation that I was on the right path.
How boring it would have been if my journey had been easy,
right? The challenges along the way are the best part; without
them, we would all be shallow, boring, very ineffective leaders,
wouldn't we? I sought out warriors who had been to hell and
back so they could show me how to navigate through my
obstacles. Nothing stood in my way.

Someone once said that more is caught than taught, and I
find this to be that truth. The things I see in my children today
are evidence of what they saw in this Cinderella's fight to get
into the palace. My fight has shown them how to navigate
the obstacles they will encounter, and I have always taught

my children that they have a destiny unique to them and to NEVER let anyone tell them that they can't do something. If they can *see it* and are willing to work for it, they can *have it.*

The boss who fired me did me a huge favor, and I will forever be grateful that in that moment I chose to rise up to the challenge and not give up. It is your choice to feed your dreams or starve them—to walk in faith or fear. My life dramatically changed just one short year after I began my own business—which the majority expected me to fail at. I think you will smile when you hear it because God has a great sense of humor. I had just been at a seminar to honor all the achievers in this business. So there I was—excited, free, and living a limitless life with so much to look forward to! I left the conference more excited than ever and had earned so many ribbons that I was displaying them proudly as if I were a county fair pig. I was WINNING! My plane ride home from the conference had a connection in Atlanta, Georgia, and this is where the fun began. So, I was coming off the plane to connect to the next one. As I looked to my right, the stooge who fired me was sitting there with his business associates. Of course they saw me, and I think the blood must have run out of their bodies for a moment because they looked like they saw a ghost from Christmas past. I walked up to them with my ribbons on—heck, I might have even had a tiara on, I was *so* happy! And you know what? I bent over, looked him in the eye, and said, "I never got to thank you for firing me."

I can only imagine that he thought, *"This woman has lost her mind! She has gone from corporate America to the loony farm with all her ribbons and tiara!"* But remember warriors don't enlist naysayers' opinions. It made my day to walk away with a great big smile.

Soon after this encounter, my business really took off, and I got married along the way to a wonderful man named Peter. Just three and a half years after the doors were shut in my face in corporate America, I was able to take cash and put it down on a beautiful lot on a lake, where I would build a 5,000 square foot home. I had so much debt, and the banks weren't going to loan me a dime on my looks, but they sure had to take notice when I gave them $40,000 for the land. I will never forget the men in their three-piece suits looking down on me like they were taking a huge chance on me. With my bad credit—plus owning my own business—it was a huge risk for them, right? WRONG. It didn't matter to me if the house went up brick by brick without a loan. It would be built, and my kids would live in the house I told them about and imagined for them to have. It took over fifteen banks until Peter and I found someone to give us a loan—and even with that, they were charging very high interest. But it was going to be built, and I knew in time the interest would be lowered.

My oldest son Nathan told me stories of what it was like riding the bus home while we were building the house. The kids would ask, "Who is building that huge house?" Nathan would smile and say, "That house is MINE!" Can you imagine my two kids, who were made fun of at one time because their single mom had no money, standing up as a warrior to say, "That house is mine"? Nathan reminds me how proud he was—and YES! WE SURE DID IT! Once again I just never doubted that the picture in my mind was the palace all along, and yours should be too. The house went up; we moved in; and my business and dream grew bigger as we welcomed another little miracle into the family—our son Sam Vrinios. Oh, those moments when we arrive where we know we belonged all along are so sweet, aren't they?

So what is your imagination telling you right now? What do you see, and what is your vision? Visions are a mental image produced by the imagination. They are intelligent foresights—a great perception of future developments. To see is to believe what is possible, to imagine, to form a mental image, to form a clear and telling picture. So what does your mental picture say to you about your MAGNIFICENCE?

As a little girl, I was always using my imagination—and not just for play, but for real. You see, it was my imagination that helped me survive a home that lacked the love a child longs for. My imagination was the very tool that God gave me to survive through life. During my days on public aid as a young adult, I just kept imagining a better life for me and my children. I never gave up on what God put in my heart because I knew He always keeps His promises.

I am addicted to faith because it works. I kept believing for more because the mental image in my mind was not the one I was living, so that is what I kept fighting for. So many people tried to convince me that I was stuck with my mistakes. They'd tell me, "Hey, you should just accept that you are a statistic, Jamie. After all, at least you're alive, right?" I don't think so! I was going to DREAM and LIVE. I was going to live out loud every step of the way.

Who would have ever imagined that a woman in my situation would end up later living in a palace, married to her prince with three beautiful, magnificent kids? Well, I did, and that is because I believed it first! The steps I took along the way of never giving in to anything less than the vision God gave me is the reason I am successful. Sure there were obstacles, but it's in our weakest moment that God is at His best. Just trust, let go, and let God take over. Keep in mind that when the pressure is on, that's when you must apply more pressure to get results. It's under the pressure—the squeeze—that God will put His "super" on your "natural."

God is waiting for a moment to show up and show off, but you have to give him something to work with. Something bigger than you, something that will live beyond your lifetime is what a dream and pursuing the MAGNIFICENT is about. There were so many people who never thought my life would turn out so beautiful, and that's what they get for thinking. Too much thinking will make you stinking.

I was told as a child, "Don't let your imagination run away with you, Jamie." I am so glad I chose to ignore that advice. I'm glad I made the decision to believe what I see and summon the courage to speak it and have the faith to jump in with my whole heart and mind. The things I have imagined have come to pass, and God continues to stretch my imagination because there is so much more to come. The power of faith and having God as your partner is one heck of a recipe to magnificence. My faith in the vision that was placed in my mind and heart is the very thing that inspired me enough to speak it and take action to think so limitlessly.

My life was literally transformed because I put a "Do Not Disturb" sign on the past and took ownership of my imagination. Keep in mind it is the person who has never done anything who is sure it can't be done. Are you going to listen to *that* voice or the very voice inside of you that keeps encouraging you to DREAM BIG? You see, your dream should be too great and vast to be measured by your life only. It is something that must extend way beyond ourselves and actually has nothing to do with us and everything to do with others.

We all have that moment where we must decide, "Am I willing to move forward toward my dream? And is the decision I make today going to lead me to the tomorrow that I actually have desired for my life?" Where will you be next week, next month, or next year? It will be totally your choice. Personally, I gave myself no other option than to finish what I started, and giving up was just not part of my DNA. I made an uncommon decision in a moment that was not perfect but absolutely necessary and required me to pursue my magnificence.

Decision is the capacity to get past any excuse in order to change any and every part of your life in an instant. It's not the condition of our lives that determines success or failure. Rather, success relies on the uncommon decision that *no matter what*, we will never give up on the dream—never! Decision precedes all action, as I've said. The important thing is not where you start; it's the decision you make about where you will end up that gives you the power to make your dreams come true. Stating a preference and making a decision are just not the same. Decision cuts off all other possibilities in order to pursue the dream. I was willing to pay the price; and quite frankly, I will continue to pursue my dreams with passion because I understand that the day I stop the pursuit is the day my life becomes stale and ineffective. I believe you can have anything in the world if you are willing to pay the price, so are you willing?

You will have to want this dream more than your fear or the excuses. You must be sold out—100%—or you will miss the mark every single time. The caterpillar has to give up crawling to emerge into a butterfly, and the same applies to leaders who are in pursuit of the magnificent. They are required to give up crawling and be radically sold on soaring with the eagles. We have many leaders in the world, but the uncommon leaders are ones who exceed that mark and operate at an exceptional mindset, accepting nothing less than what they have imagined. We must be great with being the stand-out to go against the herd and status-quo mentality, making people with small thinking VERY uncomfortable. It challenges them to grow, and most people hate the thought of change.

We live in a society where everyone is all about being comfortable and focusing on me, me, and more me; however, this is quite delusional because every living thing must grow. Keep this in mind: if it is really a dream worth pursuing, it cannot just be about me, me, and more me. My children saw me go to hell and back, but they have always known it was for them, not me. It didn't matter what was going on around me; there was no way I was ever going to let my kids down or quit on them and our dreams.

I heard a story recently of a little mouse and an elephant crossing the bridge over a very deep ravine. The elephant and the mouse crossed over the bridge, and the bridge shook. As they got to the other side, the mouse looked at his huge companion and said, "We really shook that bridge, didn't we?" Imagine that when you cross over to your magnificence, you will look up and say, "God, we really shook that finish line, didn't we?"

Remember Hebrews 11:1: "Now faith is the substance of things hoped for, the evidence of things not seen." Faith is the here and now. Here's the truth: Warriors have more faith in running over than they have in running out. I had to believe first in the dream, and that is what inspired me to take the action required to take my life from the pit to the palace. If you can *imagine it,* then you can *have it.* Zero to 65 in 2.8 seconds!

During the process of creating my business, I absolutely made choices that the average person would disagree with because most of society doesn't believe in hard work anymore. However, I actually *do* believe in focused hard work toward a bigger purpose than paying bills. I consider it a huge privilege to be healthy enough to pursue magnificence so I can help those who just straight up can't because they are in circumstances that make it impossible for them. Now, I want you to picture me: a serious, corporate single mom who had been living in a man's world and was then thrown into an environment of all women. I had no desire—at least I didn't think I did at the time—to work with women, but God had an entirely different plan for me. The moment I was placed in this arena full of powerful women, I wanted to quit—but guess what? WARRIORS NEVER QUIT!

I see a lot of women that have a passion to do something outside the home and also be with their kids, but they hold themselves back because the advice infused into their conversations are inclusive of pushing the biggest guilt trips on them just because they are a mom. So, is being a mom some kind of prison sentence? Small-minded people of the world don't understand that there can actually be an inspiring and brilliant woman who can contribute even more to her children and family outside of being home. Some women don't want to be stay-at-home moms. And guess what? It's really okay!

When I was married to my first husband, he left every single week for days to go examine banks, and I was left in a tiny little apartment pregnant and with a six-month-old child. I knew absolutely no one and had nothing going on outside the home. There is only so much baby talk a woman can do until she will lose her mind. Some moms are the CEO of the house and have given their life to their children. They find themselves watching Elmo so much that they start to act and look like Elmo—all because this is what most men think women are supposed to do. And that's ridiculous.

So the women who have given up *everything*—including their bodies—to raise a family now have a poor self-image, only to see her husband come home, flip on the TV, and look at the women on their shows, which encourages a delusional mindset about what women should actually look like. The husbands then compare those TV women to their wife—who has no makeup on and has had kids hanging on her hip all day—and we wonder why there are so many depressed women! It's pretty clear why.

I think the disrespect shown to women is quite messed up—don't you? The exploitation of women is out of control, and it is *everywhere*. We have people in society who have actually INVESTED in disempowering and degrading women. Don't even think it hasn't encouraged the sex trafficking and abuse in the world. It totally infuses the perversion in our society.

When I look around, I see countless messages that speak ever so loudly to our young girls today that women's worth is in how sexy we are, not how brilliant our minds are. The world tells us that if we get sexy and focus on our looks and not our mind, then just maybe it might make us famous or desirable or valuable for a moment ... until you get past 35, at least. I mean, where are the REAL role models who protect our girls from the lies that will leave them empty both today and in the future? Young girls look around and believe it is okay to have sex at a young age, but the people who encourage this are not there when these little girls grow into mature women and eventually realize how regretful they are with the choices they made. They realize they gave up a very huge part of themselves to someone who didn't care.

I have some truth to share after the experience I have had over the last 21 years working with women and actually hearing their heart. First, little girls and women only compromise themselves when they don't feel confident in their MAGNIFICENCE. They are seeking to be *loved!* By the way, I was one of these little girls. There isn't a woman on the planet that doesn't want to be *loved*, *respected*, and *valued* for something besides being sexy. I know you may not believe this, but I have cried tears myself and with countless very successful women who had extreme regret in the choices they made that were not empowering. The truth is that we need more men who actually believe women have more to contribute to the world than being glamorous—how about *excellence, brilliance,* and *magnificence*? We need men who actually support the woman they love in pursuit of her dream outside of raising the children—if this is what her desire is. I am fortunate to be married to a man who adores me and loves me unconditionally, and this is why WE have created a MAGNIFICENT life together.

I know many people don't want to talk about this subject, but I hear from so many women who have been deeply affected by a lack of self-confidence. I hear from women when they have gone over the edge because they have gone from feeling like a princess to feeling like the frog. They forgot who they were outside of being a mom or a sex symbol. Women lose their identity all the time in the process of birthing children or growing up. The most important thing we as mothers will ever do is raise our kids, but it's also important for fathers to raise their kids—for the children and the mother. So to all the dads, you participated in creating YOUR child, right? A family is a team, and women who want to work outside of the home need the support of the other parent to be able to pursue their dream.

I remember trying to fit into this role that people were telling me was the "right thing" to do. Every day I was baking pies, making cookies, ironing sheets, sewing, making ceramics, and heck—I was even ironing underwear because I was told that made me a great mom and wife! That is a pile of crap in my opinion. At least it was for my life and purpose. There are people who actually have a passion to cook, clean, and iron, and it gives them JOY! But personally, for me, it made me severely depressed and honestly less of a good mother. Whatever you are pursuing should bring you joy; and if you are imagining something that is going to complement your being the best mom ever, then you should do it! Your family will be happier because MOM IS HAPPY!

I remember reading about the Proverbs 31 woman; and when I started to build my business, it became my focus to enlist the women who actually had a passion and vision to be a Proverbs 31 woman. The Proverbs 31 woman is a MAGNFICENT mom, wife, and a brilliant business woman who has acquired very much success and influence. She is of great noble character. Her children call her blessed, and her husband praises her. "Many women do noble things, but the Proverbs 31 woman exceeds them all." Being a Proverbs 31 woman is not about being "perfect." It's about living life with purpose. Personally, I believe God has created all women to live out this kind of MAGNIFICENCE and EXCELLENCE. I don't care whether you agree or disagree. A woman just needs to be with women who can empower her to walk in this power.

I became intensely focused on surrounding myself with women of excellence, and that is exactly what led me to creating a team that propelled me to the pinnacle of success that has changed my life and those around me.

So let me continue with my story, what led up to an important marker of success. You need to know that resistance will come right before you get your breakthrough to a new level. It's kind of like being pregnant. If you are going to give birth to a dream, first off it must be so evident to the world that *everyone* knows you are very pregnant, and you will in fact deliver this dream—no matter what! At first, you have the dream, and it is exciting! But then about nine months later, it is getting quite uncomfortable. The due date can't be stopped, so there is no turning back or giving in. Now during the transitional phase, where there are many side effects and tons of pain, you have to keep pushing—remember … you have no choice. At this phase, if your dream is really worth giving birth to, all heck may break loose. You may ask why this would happen— simply because it is the ONLY way any warrior can develop the strength, wisdom, and courage to handle the success. You see, the journey is about who we become in the process of reaching our goals. That is evident in our transformation on the other side, which does require the warrior to evolve and grow. When we go through battles in life, we should become better people. We hope the pride, arrogance, and selfishness is just eliminated in this process, and we become more aware of contributing to others than just our own agenda.

Our hunger to grow and learn increases with this pain, and we become more spiritually evolved with each battle we endure. I am not implying that you have to go through some kind of trauma in your life to be evolved; however, I am suggesting that the qualities that won't serve you well are squeezed out in this process, and this can be painful if you are constantly guarding yourself from life. The passion required to pursue the magnificent is only ignited in overcoming obstacles for the warrior.

Just a few months from hitting my goal, every hater made themselves known to me—people even told me what a horrible mom I was and that I didn't care about my children. (You know the people who think they are helping you but don't know *anything* about you or the purpose behind your intense focus.) When your motive is to help your family and the people around you, don't ever beat yourself up. The small-minded, wimpy people who never want to get uncomfortable will question you or give their non-expert opinions on the birth of your dream.

I had an intense commitment in showing my children that what we imagine ourselves to be and live out, we *absolutely* can attain. This was really significant to me because it would provide the security I wanted for my family while delivering the ultimate message to my children and the leaders who I had the privilege to mentor—that anything you believe and are willing to take action on every single day is possible. If people really believe in what they see in their mind, they will be given all the energy, resources, relationship, and focus needed to reach their destination. It all comes back to whether or not you really believe it because when you *really* believe it, the instant action is there.

Keep in mind that my two oldest children were watching this whole thing play out from the very beginning—from overcoming poverty in the first place. It was unacceptable for me to quit trying to attain my dream. The message that I would have projected to them by giving up would be that a destiny, a dream, the magnificence we have been created for—that we have imagined ourselves to be—it's just not possible, so it's okay to be like everyone else. There was no way I was going to teach my children the lesson of quitting and following the wimps who were around us in all arenas. I think by now you can figure out by my story that I declared WAR on quitting or giving in since I took my first breath. And if you haven't done that yourself, well then do it now if you want to be a warrior. I've always had an intense passion to teach my children that there is an assignment on their life that is exclusive to them. And guess what—it's unique to every one of us.

Contrary to what most people thought, EVERYTHING that was motivating me to get to where I was going was all about my family and helping others—so really, I just removed myself from anyone who wasn't on board because I was about to give BIRTH. I am so extremely grateful that my husband Peter encouraged me to win at all costs. He never left my side—in fact, he quit his job in support of *our dream* so he could help with the children. I remember when we went to return his car to Nissan, and the owner said, "You'll be back."

I just replied, "He will never be back, Bob. Thanks though." When we walked out of the store together, I'm sure they were taking bets on how fast we would fail, but that was not possible because we knew the birthing date was non-negotiable for us—no matter what. Can you imagine handing your keys in at your job in pursuit of the magnificent? You can totally do it! Also having a warrior mentor was *vital* to helping Peter and I navigate through this. Because he knew how much Marilyn had given me as a mentor, there was never interference. Peter understood that I was getting advice from a warrior who actually won the battle. And I was in the *middle of winning.*

We were on the way to church one day, and our family was going back and forth about what we should or shouldn't do regarding something in the business. Little Sammy, who was maybe four years old at the time, said, "I think we should call Marilyn and ask her." From the mouth of a babe ... It was a great lesson though. Always get advice from people who are the *experts*. I mean, do you get advice from your hair designer on how to build your home? I think not!

The journey was INTENSE! And finally the moment came to celebrate my victory. Every warrior completely understands this kind of moment because this is what all champions operate and live for.

I want to tell you the story about a beautiful night that was absolutely worth every "no," every single insult, all the quitters who quit on me, the so-called "experts" who guaranteed I would fail. The night was quite elegant, just as I had envisioned it—like a beautiful wedding. Women and men of excellence filled the room. These Proverbs 31 women and men had partnered with me and my family and were able to bless their families and others because they believed in excellence, in the magnificent. I had already been envisioning this night, and it was all finally coming together. We talked about it for years to come.

After dinner, one by one, warrior after warrior got up and shared their victory over average. Of course, the woman who I owed it all to was there—my beautiful warrior magnificent, Marilyn. It was time for my children to share, and my daughter Amber who had been away at college spoke first. She pulled out this bear with angel wings on it and told everyone that

I was her "earth angel." Amber had recorded a message into the bear to remind me while she was at school how much she loved me. Amber began to read one of the many letters that I had given her when she was growing up, encouraging her to pursue her dreams. I really never knew Amber had kept all these messages until this MAGNIFICENT night, and I am so glad she decided to share with everyone who was present that in life, *more will be caught than taught.*

I remember when I began this pursuit that Amber was only in first grade. She wrote me a letter that said, "You can be number 1 Mom, love your girl." I still have that little note today. Funny how we keep those little messages, huh? My daughter, to this day, thanks me for being that encourager in her life. I know there were many mistakes I made like any parent, but I guess there was a whole lot I did pretty magnificent to see my daughter get up and share her heart with this room full of warriors. At this point, everyone was already crying. Then my son Nathan got up to make his presentation. He was leaving right after this celebration on a trip to Honduras, but it was important to him that he shared in this MAGNIFICENT moment with his mom. After all, Nathan was always beside me the entire journey, so I knew he wouldn't miss it. Nathan stood up, six foot, four inches tall in his white tuxedo, and started to read a description of what it was like when he was a little boy and when I was a single mom.

He read the words he spoke to me when he was a child, and a few were piercing: "Mommy, do I have to grow up? I don't want to grow up. Do I ever have to leave home? Because

I never ever want to. Can I always call you Mommy? Mommy, will you sing to me 'Somewhere over the Rainbow'?" You see, all of my kids had a song, and Nathan's was "Somewhere over the Rainbow."

He had given the DJ that very special song, which we shared every night. My handsome son came over to me and took me out on the dance floor in front of hundreds of people and danced with me to the very song I sang to him as a little boy. I will never forget when he told me just how proud he was of me. With nobody else on the floor, it was just our moment celebrating the journey WE had pursued to the MAGNIFI-CENT on the other side—our rainbow. Everyone wants to *believe*, but very few ever find the courage to pursue their somewhere over the rainbow, and that is tragic. There was not a dry eye in the room after my two children presented me those priceless gifts—once-in-a-lifetime moments that will stay with me forever. Those moments were worth every single battle that I went through in my pursuit to get over the rainbow and to the other side. Let me ask you a question: If you knew you couldn't fail, how RADICAL would you allow yourself to imagine? Do you think for one second I would ever let any obstacle in my life prevent me from experiencing this kind of moment? No way!

Of course by this time, Peter was wishing he had gone before my children. Even though he got up and presented me with a beautiful mink coat, it couldn't compare to my children expressing their love and gratitude about having a mother who taught them how to WIN by her example. I *loved* my coat—but I'm just saying that it can't compare.

My example to be a woman of my word and follow what was in my heart without any excuses was and will be the greatest GIFT I will ever pass on to my children. I have demonstrated with my life that whatever God has placed in your MIND—imagination—is most definitely worth pursuing. It is the reason we are given life in the first place.

To this day, when I share that night with an audience, I see the tears fall from their eyes because I know they can feel the *true purpose* behind their hard work. They are so glad that a warrior gave them permission to pursue their dreams with ZERO apology for excellence. You can always look at the fruit in a person's life. If there is a rotten root, there is no fruit; however, a healthy root will manifest some beautiful fruit that nobody—not even the biggest naysayers of all—can negate because it is just that evident. The greatest gift we will ever pass to our children, grandchildren, nieces, nephews, and each other is to PURSUE THE MAGNIFICENT and make it so obvious to the world that no matter what, you will give birth to this dream because we are born to be MAGNIFICENT! The choices I made daily didn't lead me to just one moment. In fact, there is a lifetime of priceless memories. In the last 21 years, I have traveled all over the world in so many countries that I couldn't I even remember them all unless I really sat down to count them.

The vision that set my heart on fire to dream big, gave me the guts to pursue the magnificent, and allowed me the opportunities to travel all over the world most definitely has come true, and I am only getting started. I've had the honor to be in countries like the Ukraine and Germany to meet with women that have faith enough to take action toward what they have imagined their life to be, even in the most challenging conditions. The opportunity for me to get up in front of thousands and share my story was given to me because I WON the battle many of them were in the middle of. It all goes back to *we win the battle so we can help others win too.* People follow successful people in life, and there is no way around it. If we want to contribute outside of our own lives into other people's lives, we must win! What a huge privilege I have, all because I believed in my somewhere over the rainbow—imagination.

I remember one of the most significant moments in my life was when I was training in the Ukraine. Peter and I were there, and I was given the opportunity to share my heart. I could feel that my message was connecting with the women on a very deep level. These leaders were so open to the message of making a difference in other people's lives and living out their MAGNIFICENCE to the point that I could have trained for hours, and I bet they would have gone without food and water to hear it, as I would have. You see, nothing is more empowering to a warrior than to be given an opportunity to pour into the hungry young warriors who are going to apply what they were just fed. We can feed 1,000 people the same meal of knowledge—why is it that some people will grow, yet some still starve when it comes to leadership?

It comes down to HEART. So many people get it backward because they think more training is the answer. In truth, they just need to infuse their imagination. The systems, training, and information are completely useless if the imagination is left uninspired and our heart is not connecting with people. When the imagination is working at its optimal rate, we will attract everything and everyone necessary to manifest the magnificent. It's like first making an imprint with permanent marker in the mind that connects us to everything necessary for us to reach our dreams. We must imagine it FIRST and allow ourselves to connect to the people who are destined to be on the journey with us.

We had been in the Ukraine for two days when we attended a reception with some very influential warriors. It was amazing. Peter and I were asked a question that really touched us both to the core. "Was it love at first sight?" At first, we were kind of caught off guard, but we both smiled and replied, "Yes." We were speaking through an interpreter, and she said the Ukrainian women wanted us to know that they knew it was. They said they could tell how much Peter loved me by the way he treated me and showed respect to me. Think about this for a moment—again more is caught by our example than anything we could ever speak. We knew that their hearts were captured from all the love that was exuding—not just from my training—but the very relationship with my man.

Let me ask you a question: When you met your imagination for the first time, was it love at first sight? When we meet something that touches our spirit deep down, we know it, right? The same happens with our imagination. We can immediately start over-thinking the connection, or we can just accept it as truth. Most people will immediately let doubt enter their mind, but my advice is to never entertain that second thought because it will lead to disbelief in what is supposed to be. Follow that deep-down feeling you know is truth for you.

It is your truth and only yours because it is unique to your gifts. If you have seen the love and purpose of your life at some point, and to this day you can remember the first moment you met with this picture placed in your mind, then what are you going doing do with it? If it really was love at first sight, isn't it worth the pursuit? It must be love, and that is what people should see all over you without a word being said.

You + Magnificence = Must be True Love

Why would we treat our purpose with less respect and love than what we would expect from the man or woman we choose to spend a lifetime with? Don't you think it should be obvious to everyone that your MAGNIFICENCE was indeed "love at first sight"? Remember when I shared with you the moment I delivered my children? And it was that very LOVE I kept going back to that reminded me of my magnificence? Can you sit down long enough with the TV off, your cell phone down, and nobody around and find your first love—that forever imprint designed uniquely for you and only you? When you find it, your entire world will be transformed if you handle it with tender loving care and a deep, profound respect.

I am so glad I found it and was given the gift of a lifetime to share my heart with those beautiful women in the Ukraine, and I know there are so many more countries I will visit to share this message of the warrior who dared to imagine and fall in love with her magnificence. Now it's time for YOU to do the same. So get your crayons out and get the paint brushes in your hand because the canvas is as bright as you choose it to be. Just trust the imprint placed in your mind. We have the power to imagine the pit or the palace. *Your life, your choice, your dream. Dream and live* or *doubt and die.*

Since we are on the topic of unleashing our imaginations, I must share with you the success stories of my two sons. You see, I know both of them were encouraged to unleash their imagination and the entrepreneur inside of them because I passed this down by unleashing mine first. Both of them were able to have confidence in what they could see in their imagination, which was unique to both. Nathan, who is now 28, started his business immediately after graduating college. Even though he received a degree in finance and business, he chose to work for himself. His vision was unstoppable—to build his company VE Websites. Nathan was discouraged by almost everyone around him. The expert opinion was your typical status-quo advice of "You should get a job. It's secure."

If you really think about that statement, you realize it is false because nothing is 100% secure. Everything involves risk. Warriors are willing to take the risk involved in developing their vision—imagination, company, and their contribution— all because they are just that confident in what they have first imagined in their minds. Nathan was sold out, ready to move his life from 0 to 65 in 2.8 seconds—no matter what. It has been absolutely amazing to watch him build his company from the ground into a very successful business. I assure you that his mentoring and example of success as an entrepreneur played a huge role in inspiring his little brother Sam, who is now 16, to develop his company at the age of 14. Does it get any more powerful than this—two brothers unleashing the entrepreneurial spirit within!

Nathan went into battle first—completely fearless, unstoppable with no excuses, and determined to WIN so other people could WIN. And that is exactly what he did. He is the owner of VE Websites. Now we have Sam, this young warrior entrepreneur who thinks his brother is right up there next to God. After all, I have been self-employed Sam's entire life, and Nathan has now proven how easy this is. So, Sam thought, *"Why not?"* You see, hanging around warrior entrepreneurs who infuse their creativity and imagination into others makes things seem simple and easy, inspiring them to believe and unleash their own greatest potential.

So Sam, at the age of 14, decided he would start his company Imagine Controllers, which designs any gaming controllers that you can imagine. Imagine Controllers' slogan is "You imagine it, and we will create it." Ironically, both of my sons developed their companies in the middle of the recession over the last few years. Think about that, and IMAGINE it for just one minute. Two sons who saw their mom win in owning her own business and pursuing MAGNIFICENCE, and both were inspired by the win—Nathan first, who by his example and win also inspired his baby brother to win too.

When we think about a legacy, it is most definitely inclusive of all the qualities we were able to transfer to others; and with each generation, it should grow stronger. This is why we MUST WIN—so the transfer can happen and the MAGNIF-ICENCE will grow stronger in our children and then their children. Leadership is *succession,* leaving a legacy that will continue after we are gone. It is just that simple. So if nobody can replicate what you are teaching, it will never lead to a legacy. Without a legacy, anything we want to pass on will die and be deemed worthless because there was nobody to carry on the magnificence.

Imagination, vision, belief, winning, love, and two WAR-RIOR MAGNIFICENTS—two entrepreneurs who imagined 0 to 65 in 2.8 seconds—so they did it. The legacy will go on and on because when they believed enough to pursue what they saw in their minds actually happen.

Legacy – "More is caught than taught."

If you have zero desire to pursue excellence in life, there is absolutely no reason to continue reading this book. If you are getting bored at reading a chapter or a few sentences, you really should stop reading because this information won't help until you make the choice to WIN every single day. If the opinions of naysayers actually matter to you, then you will probably get excited for a minute, but you will choose to ignore advice that summons you to transform. However, if the opinions of the herd make zero impact on you, then you are ready for the truthful, fearless conversations that only a WARRIOR has a desire to engage in.

A leader who sees and commits to his imagination and refuses to quit will win and pass this on to those around them. This requires you to believe that what you see in your mind is *truth*. You must dream big, imagine big, and surround yourself with faith giants so you can acquire the DNA of a warrior, or there is no possibility of a win. The ACTION you take or choose to not take will speak so loudly that absolutely nothing else needs to be said. You must expect and demand the magnificent if you want to live in the MAGNIFICENT.

Our lives as we know them are a direct result of the thoughts we think and the words we speak, leading to the actions we have or have not taken in the moment. Many leaders want success, but they are not willing to pay the price because they are limited by their thinking, in turn limiting the actions they take. If you speak to any successful leader, he or she will tell you that there is a price for success. You can label it your dream, purpose, calling, MAGNIF-ICENCE, or the FIRE that burns within—either way, it is deep inside every warrior, and it is a choice to rise up and win or walk away.

God doesn't change His mind about destiny. He is not going to put a dream in a your heart and not give you every-thing it takes to finish. God never quits on us; we quit on God because it gets too uncomfortable. You don't like the squeeze? Get over it and get up and fight! YOUR dream will not come at bargain prices, meaning that you will be inconvenienced and uncomfortable. You will make the people around you that have limited thinking very uncomfortable. You will have to work hard, and you will have to summon faith and you will have to make a decision that your purpose and your passion are bigger than anything that life is throwing at you. You can't be in neutral and pursue the MAGNIFICENT. You must decide if you want to be on the sideline of life while continuing to make excuses or to get up and freaking FIGHT! Choose to take your life from 0 to 65 in 2.8 seconds.

Nobody follows a quitter or someone who makes excuses! They follow a warrior. Warriors win and conquer their deepest fears because they are the real deal. Anyone who is in a warrior's presence knows this: You can't fake passion or vision; you either have it or you don't. Vision can only come from God because He knows exactly what we are created for. So instead of questioning your MAGNIFICENCE, could we all agree it is time to live in our MAGNIFICENCE? Don't get to the finish and have regret while others say, "Gosh, I wish I had." I know ... God forbid somebody actually speak the truth about success because you know what? It's not easy. It's not convenient. But to all of you who admire the conquerors in life, ask any of us if it is worth it. I can say, "OH YES, YES, YES ... IT IS!!"

Seriously I look around and ask myself, *"Where are the warriors with passion and conviction about who they are and where they are going?"* Seriously, is it that easy to toss a leader back and forth like the waves of a sea? Actually, it is if the leader is double-minded and not clear about what he or she sees and wants.

It's not possible to stop leaders who know that they *know* that they KNOW what they want and believe what God has placed in their heart and mind. To all the warriors who are still reading this, you will always be brought to the edge before you will see God show up and show off suddenly. I have *never* seen any great warrior coast into the finish line. If you coasted, then your MAXIMUM POTENTIAL has not been met, and you could have exceeded what you thought was possible—exceedingly, abundantly anything we ever dreamed or imagined.

You must see it, and you must believe it and accept it as true and real. You must have confidence and trust in what God has put in your heart and mind. He always finishes what He starts, so stop entertaining doubt and be bold enough to speak it out. And remember: you can't have the things you speak against in life, so STOP speaking against the dream you are destined to live out. Stop saying "I can't; I don't know; and I hope so." Start speaking words of life into yourself and those around you. Remember your words will tell on you, and speaking your dream out loud means you actually have confidence in what you believe.

Many dreams die because the dreamer lacks the confidence to declare them. Whenever we are unsure of ourselves, we remain silent. A warrior speaks out boldly and fearlessly, so speak up so you can be heard without hesitation. Your words will bring life or death—choose to speak life to your dreams and magnificence.

Your action is a reflection of your faith. What do your actions say about you? Are you a hearer or a doer? A doer is someone who moves beyond his imagination and into action. Is that you?

John Maxwell said:

A. Doers are not lazy.

B. Doers are willing to work in whatever circumstances are necessary.

C. Doers are willing to change and exchange old methods for new.

D. Doers are proud of what they have accomplished, but they aren't satisfied with stopping there.

E. Doers do.

F. Doers make the world go 'round. We write about them; we talk about them; we are amazed at their focus, tenacity, and accomplishment. What do doers have? DETERMINATION.

Determined thoughts have passion and intent behind them. Determined thoughts make you *believe* what it takes, *say* what it takes, and even *change* whatever it takes to start living in your MAGNIFICENCE. Nothing will be restrained from those who have imagined what they will do! There is nothing you can't accomplish.

The only way to discover the limits of the possible is to go beyond them into impossible.

Get rid of the exit signs in your life. As long as there is a way out, you will be tempted to take it rather than pay the price. The more you walk by faith, the more you will hear from the doubters. Just remember that the person who has never done anything is the one who is sure it can't be done.

STAND BY ME

The greatest privilege in the world is when a master warrior—a warrior magnificent—who is stronger than you, wiser than you, and more experienced than you, sends you the rare invitation to stand by them. Accepting this invitation guarantees a victory. This book is your invitation. Stand by ME, and the win will happen—the battle will be won. You can count on that! How can a warrior say this to someone they are mentoring? I can tell you how and why. It's because that warrior has won battle after battle and has a vast amount of wisdom. Warriors who mentor others have mastered the comeback after being in the darkest of nights, so they *know* eventually they will win the battle—but only if they refuse to give in to the challenges presented, the pressure, the squeeze—the opportunity to see what is in this great warrior.

Have you ever been given the rare invitation to stand by a warrior? If not, has it not been proposed to you because the message and energy you are sending is, "Don't count on me; count on someone else"? I'm just throwing that out there to all the warriors who really want to be truthful with themselves. WARRIOR MAGNIFICENTS only ask warriors to stand by and stand up with them because they know that warrior will win and not back down—no matter what. The warrior who taps you on the shoulder and asks you to get in the game isn't asking you because he or she *hopes* you will get a touchdown. That warrior is counting on you to play full-out and get the *winning touchdown*. He knows you can do it.

In a mentorship, the moment will come when you are given the privilege of demonstrating all that the WARRIOR MAGNIFICENT has taught you, the protégé. You see, if you are going to stand by a warrior magnificent—the coach and mentor—that person expects to see his investment in you pay off. That opportunity will always present itself when the warrior magnificent knows you are ready to take the ball. Mentors are seeking a player who will pass on what their mentor—*their* warrior magnificent—taught them. This is the legacy we talked about earlier.

I've talked a little about my mentor of 20 years and what she did for me. The greatest gift that could have ever been returned to her was the winning touchdown. When the moment came, she said, "It's time. The time is now, Jamie. I'm expecting you to give me a return on my investment."

If you were ever privileged enough to be under a champion coach, you know exactly what I am referring to. For a champion coach, excellence is absolutely expected, or you won't be put in the game. Let me give you a quick story before I elaborate on what I did for love. Our son Sam plays football for the number one high school football team in the state of Florida. His coach is known as a champion coach—and everyone clearly knows this. Sam realized that in order to play on this quality of a team, especially with a warrior magnificent mentoring him, he would have to prove to the coach he was ready to perform, or there would be *zero* opportunities ever given to him. On a champion football team like this, it really only takes just ONE opportunity to get the attention of colleges for a scholarship. College scouts know this coach has trained excellent players to be warriors.

Sam has told me story after story of how this coach operates and the skill level he expects out of the players in the game. The same is true in life outside of sports. A warrior magnificent will have extremely high standards and refuse to compromise at any cost, as warriors know that compromise leads to average performance. Warriors have no interest in average, so an attitude of "just good enough" won't work with a champion mentor. As many have said, "Good enough is the enemy of excellence."

If warriors are under leadership that is average, they will stop listening and following that average coach because they can sense this mentor is not a warrior. It just doesn't work. Warriors can sense that the average, herd mentality will never be strong enough to lead them *anywhere*, much less in winning a freaking battle. We as warriors must have a warrior magnificent summon the excellence from within and go beyond what we could ever have dreamed possible and help drive us into the MAGNFICENT.

With Sam's football experience the year prior having been under an average coach, and now being in the presence of a WARRIOR coach, he found himself being challenged beyond what he thought was his potential. This is what we want to achieve when we choose a mentor. I will never forget the day Sam shared with me what his coach said to him a little before the first opportunity Sam was given to play. The coach told Sam, "Stand by me. Just stand by me, Sam, and you will be given the opportunity when it's time." I wish you could have seen Sam's face while he was telling me this story. He was *so* excited.

The big game night finally came. As I sat in the stands, I focused on Sam on the sidelines as he watched the plays. I knew Sam was hoping he had proven to the coach that he was ready and had earned the right to play on the field with this champion team. Sure enough, that moment came. He had *one shot* to run the ball and perform—and that is exactly what he did. This win instilled confidence in Sam—but even more so, this WIN showed that his coach believed enough in him to give him the ball. All warriors want the ball and are waiting for the warrior coach to send them the priceless invitation to "stand by me." And I promise you, the opportunity to run the ball is going to happen.

So again, let me ask you this: have you put yourself in a position to be given such an invite? Or are you still hiding in the back of the classroom, hoping the teacher doesn't ask you a question about the homework from the night before? You see, the warrior has done his homework *daily* and is ready to be asked the question. But more importantly, the warrior is ready to *pass the test*.

The warrior isn't hiding in the back of the room or sitting on the bench eating donuts while everyone else is sweating their guts out to win the game. The warrior is passionately STANDING by the coach—so hungry to just get in the game and get on the green. Young warriors know that their moments will happen if they keep showing up to practice and giving their mentors and team 100% of what they have. We can't expect to be given the ball without giving that 100% because giving even just 99% means you will miss that opportunity.

Imagine going into a major surgery and hearing the doctor operating on you say, "Hey, I'm tired today so I'm not going to give it 100%. I might let you die on the table." A lot of leaders who want to be warriors will never reach their MAGNIFI-CENCE because they are not willing to throw it down 100% every single day. Instead, they let their dreams die on the table. The very first step to even attracting the right mentor is some-thing I've already mentioned, and that is TRUST—trust in the vision that God has placed in your spirit and mind, and open your heart to the process of how this will be manifested.

For me personally, God sent the perfect champion coach at a very critical time in my life. And guess what! I was hungry as always for *growth*. I was open and willing to embrace everything she had to offer me. Remember me? I was in the pit. So in my mind, there was clearly only one way I could go—and that was UP, UP, UP to the palace where all Cinderellas belong.

Can you summon this much trust in both your vision and your coach? Are you willing to immediately apply any instruc-tion given by your mentor? The teacher really does appear when the warrior is ready and hungry to receive what he or she is there to offer.

If someone wants to transform his physical body and health, he doesn't sign up for a friendly membership to a gym—that is only for the herd. A WARRIOR will seek out a champion coach—the most EXCELLENT trainer who will summon the greatness within him and bring transformation.

This concept applies to all areas of our lives. When we desire truth and transformation, only then will we be delivered the mentor and given the rare "stand-by-me" invitation from the warrior who has the key to having our destiny fulfilled. You must be willing and open to the truth if you want to see full manifestation of your magnificence.

The value of this mentor is priceless in a warrior's life. A warrior magnificent will cut down the learning curve and empower you in ways that you couldn't have even imagined. When your champion warrior appears to get you through the battle, will you be ready to accept the invite? Or will you be sitting there solely focused on getting by and surviving—really living in doubt instead of pursuing the magnificent? Remember that your mentor will know if you are ready—and believe me, nothing has to even be said because your attitude and energy is apparent without any WORDS being spoken.

A great mentor isn't there to be your best friend. The mentor is placed in your life to take you to a new level, whereas a best friend will always give you permission to be comfortable. Best friends will act like they get it; but unless they have been through it themselves, guess what? They don't get it! Let's just be truthful. Best friends can be wonderful cheerleaders, but they can never be the coach a warrior must have to take the victory. Iron sharpens iron, and a warrior mentor will bring out uncommon warrior magnificence that is rare.

I really do contribute who I am today to my warrior magnificent Marilyn. She was a treasured gift in my life. There is no possible way that I could have gotten through the many obstacles in my life without her unconditional love and belief in me. She has been the most precious gift I could have ever received on my journey.

This past March, my warrior magnificent Marilyn passed away of cancer. Every single day that has passed since, I have realized more and more the great significance and role she played in my life and my magnificence. The conversations that we had daily and weekly have left me forever changed. Now that she is no longer here to talk to me, I realize why God chose Marilyn to be the one to love me to success.

Even today, there are so many moments I wish I could call her up and tell her about all the wonderful things that are happening. She was always standing for me in all that I pursued. We can never take our mentors for granted nor the time they are in our lives to call out our magnificence. Those priceless conversations I had with Marilyn will last me a lifetime and will continue to contribute to my success. The value of such a mentor is limitless.

I can assure you that I never questioned her, and I always trusted the process of this mentor's purpose in my life. If she had told me to eat dirt, I would have willingly done it! I knew that anything she encouraged me to do would only make me better in all areas of my life. Breakthrough to the magnificent and *optimal* performance in the field—with outrageous and audacious determination—can't happen without the trust in a warrior mentor. We can't trust mentors, however, until we learn first to trust in ourselves. Again it goes back to that thing really deep inside us, stirring for the warrior to believe enough to STAND.

I read a story a long time ago that had a profound impact on me. I'm sure you have heard a version of this same story as well, but I want to share with you my version. At the end, you will most definitely know whether or not you are a warrior. In fact, it will be evident whether or not you are a warrior eagle.

One day, a warrior eagle egg rolled into a chicken coop. (Don't ask me HOW it got there because that's not a question I can answer for you!) Anyway, soon after, this little egg hatched into a baby eagle. All the chickens immediately started laughing at this little bird because she was different from them. The little eagle was so confused. After all, she was birthed into this chicken coop, right? So this must be where she belongs! Every day, the little eagle would go through so many battles and ask herself, *"Why am I so different? Why are these other chickens labeling me a 'misfit' and rejecting me?"*

This little eagle would walk outside the coop and stare into the sky, only to find herself imagining something more magnificent than what she had now. This little bird would actually have thoughts come into her mind like, *"Hey, did you know you can SOAR?"*

The little eagle would always get this stirring deep down inside her every single time she left the coop, and it encouraged her to DREAM about taking flight and soaring. But the minute she walked back into the coop house, her dreams were dampened as everyone reminded her that she was insignificant to the other chickens. One day, a warrior walked into this farmer's chicken coop while the farmer was working, and the warrior said to the farmer, "Did you know that little bird is not a chicken? Did you know that is a rare eagle?"

Well, the farmer laughed at this warrior and said, "Seriously? Are you crazy? That bird is a chicken. She walks like a chicken and chirps like the other chickens. That is hilarious!"

The warrior replied with complete confidence, "You are absolutely wrong. I know an eagle when I see one. I am going to take this little eagle under my mentorship and teach her to soar." The farmer didn't care because he saw no purpose in keeping this defective bird around, so the warrior invited that baby eagle to stand by her. Of course the baby eagle said yes.

The warrior breathed belief into this little eagle daily, encouraging her and telling her she was born to soar. The little eagle gleaned from every action the warrior demonstrated, and a strong confidence grew daily. The fierce trust and loyalty in the warrior was evident by the little eagle's immediate response to instruction on how to soar.

Days and months went by as this little warrior eagle grew in beauty, confidence, and love for the gift deep within to soar. The moment soon came when the fierce warrior brought this little eagle back to the chicken coop to see if she had any desire at all to live among the chickens. The eagle declared that she most definitely did not belong with the chickens.

You see, it was clear to her now that she was nothing like those chickens. The magnificence was evident to her—and all the chickens now—by the very presence she carried with her as a warrior eagle. The warrior knew it was time to see the protégé eagle soar and invited her to walk to the highest mountain they could find. As they walked side by side, this warrior mentor continued to remind her protégé of all the things she taught her about the very magnificence the eagle was destined to live out. The warrior assured the eagle that she was ready to soar.

The warrior magnificent knew when they got to the top of this mountain that the final moment to challenge the little eagle warrior to soar would present itself. The moment finally arrived, and the warrior magnificent took the little warrior eagle in her arms and said, "Little eagle, I *believe* in you, I *love* you, and I *know* you can SOAR!"

At first the young warrior eagle was afraid; but when she looked into the eyes of her warrior magnificent, the eagle was reminded of all the things she was given and embraced her magnificence to soar. The warrior magnificent pushed the eagle off the mountain. And guess what the young warrior eagle did? You are right! She soared and soared, just like she had imagined. In fact, it was *beyond* what she imagined.

If you want to soar, then you have to get away
from the chickens in life.
Be prepared and ready for the invite to stand
by and stand up with the warriors.

Just like Sam and this little eagle, my coach, mentor, and warrior magnificent tapped me on the shoulder and said, "Get on the green, Jamie. It's time to SOAR. I'm counting on you to win!" I will never forget that day; and if a master warrior like this has ever tapped you on the shoulder, consider it the greatest compliment in your life because he or she saw enough and believed enough in you to put you in the game. It's a privilege to be asked to play on a team of warriors. This was not a comfortable moment for me, but it was owed with interest because of all that she poured into me. I absolutely owed it to her to get the touchdown.

I remember when she expected me and a few other warriors to get on the green and win the game. It was our very last opportunity to play the game with her as our warrior coach. Let me say this: Had we not won this game, her message and all that she had invested in us would have never spread past the bench—and we all know that no one listens to the players who are sitting on the bench. Players on the bench have no interest in wining, so they are never given the once-in-a-lifetime invitation to "stand by me." The choice is yours—stand or sit. Will you stand with a warrior magnificent or sit down with the players and chickens who are eating donuts, never even interested in an invitation to pursue the magnificent?

FIERCE AND UNWAVERING

All through our lives we are influenced by the people we accept or decline invitations from daily. This can serve as a powerful asset in attaining the magnificent, or it will detour you from even getting on the green. When Sam was little, and Amber and Nathan were teenagers, we were getting ready to purchase our second home in Florida, which is where I always wanted to live. After nine years of daily, consistent, 100% focus and discipline, we were finally about to move into our house near the ocean. As a side note, I have always known I would live there because I *imagined it first*, so it is where my mind has requested me to be.

While we were in the pursuit this new home, we stayed at one of the hotels on the beach in Longboat Key. We had stayed there a few times before, and we always stayed in the President suite, so the ocean was just a few steps from our room. One morning, when Sam was about five years old, he and I were taking a walk on the beach. He was quite wise for a little guy, so the questions were endless. Sammy had just heard from the staff at our hotel that the room we stayed in was the exact same room that the United States President had slept in. To a five-year-old, this rocked his world and definitely expanded his vision.

We have always taught Sam that you are who you hang around, and whatever energy they have on them—whether good or bad—will rub off on you. We taught him to surround himself with people who will sharpen him in life. With that in mind, Sammy looked up at me and said, "Mommy, you have taste just like the President, don't you?"

I replied "Yes, I do Sam. We must like the same things."

Sammy said, "You are as important as the President too!" Of course I replied, "You're right!"

He went on to say, "Mommy, the room we are sleeping in is where the president has slept. So tonight, I'm going to get in that bed where he slept because I want some of that to rub off all over me!"

Can you believe that? He was right though. Whatever mentors we choose—or the mentors that choose us—will have a profound impact on our MAGNIFICENCE. You better make sure whoever you surround yourself with and take advice from is someone you want to, as Sammy said it, "rub off all over you."

As a little girl, I had great warriors who coached me to be excellent in all that I pursued, whose best traits rubbed off on me. Let's start with my father and mother who disowned me almost 30 years ago. I can tell you this: I saw excellence in being the daughter of a doctor who got up early to read every day before he performed surgery and was disciplined in all areas of his life. For that example, I am forever grateful. My mother always presented herself with an image of excellence and made sure all six of us were dressed perfectly as the children of a doctor. My mother had to be excellent if she was going to keep order in a house with six children and a demanding husband.

I look back on my childhood and the last 30 years with gratefulness and love because I know that my parents gave me the best they were equipped to give, and it only propelled me to be the most MAGNIFICENT version of myself that I could have ever imagined to be possible. All the battles I have had victory over in the last 30 years of my life has only summoned and ignited the WARRIOR MAGNIFICENT in me.

However, this would have never been discovered without overcoming some of the deepest battle scars. It has infused me with a passion and fearlessness to help others win their battles too. I guess instead of getting addicted to something that would destroy me, I harnessed it to an addiction to *love* and to *inspire* other warrior eagles to SOAR. The WARRIOR MAG-NIFICENTS that entered my life to help me win the battles would have never had a reason to invite me to stand if my life had been perfect and never required me to win a battle.

The other warriors I had growing up were many in number—Sunday school teachers, youth group leaders, my piano teacher, pastors of my church, school teachers, my voice coach, my pageant coach, and my track coach—I guess I had a whole lot of coaching, didn't I? Do you know how grateful I am for those champion coaches, who spoke life into me daily while I was in that chicken coop, wondering if I really could soar with the eagles? You see, they knew deep down what was going on at home and why I was constantly achieving to be in their space. They each gave me an invite to stand by them because deep down those warriors knew I was a little eagle, and the chicken coop was only temporary. They knew that teaching me to win in their area of expertise would help me overcome future battles that would lead me to the MAGNIFICENT.

I'll never forget the day I met my first little warrior, my daughter Amber Rae—the little girl I dreamed about even as a child. Then just 14 months later, I held Nathan in my arms—my second little warrior. I was reminded of God's MAGNFICENCE. These two little warriors literally saved my life just by their very lives. They are an in-my-face, bold, daily reminder that God never made anyone less than magnificent. It was a reminder of the very gift of giving birth to my children and the opportunity to love the way God intended for children to be loved.

Then there were my warrior professors in college who wanted to help me get my degree even thought I was a single mom, so they made exceptions for me or assisted me in different ways to help get through the battle of my education. I had one professor who allowed me to bring my children into his office at special times for exams, and he would make balloon animals to entertain Amber and Nathan. He did that because he *knew* that I was a warrior and he was the warrior magnificent assigned to help me through that battle. You know those people who just get it without you having to say a word? These warriors know. They sense that you are a warrior, and they are there to teach and mentor you on something you need to live MAGNIFICENTLY!

Then there were the warrior employers who hired me as an inexperienced single mom. Many people with more experience wanted that medial sales position, but the warrior who was assigned to me sent me the invite to "stand by me." You see, it wasn't the education or experience the company was looking for. It was the hunger to be a *champion!* Like I said earlier, warriors can sense another warrior because of the invisible message we send.

Then, there is Peter. His name describes him perfectly—it means "rock." There is no perfect relationship in life; if you think there is, then be ready for huge disappointment. But, when we fall in love with our magnificence, we can commit to a relationship that becomes the wind beneath our wings. Peter has always been this for me, and I will be forever grateful for his patience, his unconditional love, and his belief in me. I remember that so many people told me all the reasons that Peter wasn't for me, but they were wrong, just like all the other "experts." I have been asked the question, "Why Pete? Why did you pick Pete?"

My reply is always, "Peter loves me *unconditionally*, and I know without a shadow of a doubt that he will never leave my side." One night, my mentor Marilyn even crowned him "Man of the Year." I will never forget the moment he shared about his love for me and how the entire audience was moved by his fierce love for me and our family. He told them that when he met me, all I had was God. He just couldn't believe that someone would actually disown a young, single mom. And if it took him the rest of his life to prove to me that he loves me and will never leave me, then that is what he will do. And you know what? He has kept his word. I couldn't be anywhere *near* the woman, mom, friend, or business professional I am today if it wasn't for my rock of a warrior Peter. Yep, it was love at first sight, and it always will be.

Then there was the birth of Sammy, my mighty little warrior who continues to infuse this family with pure love and an unleashed imagination. Seeing my two sons walking in their warrior magnificence together—sharpening each other like iron sharpening iron—is quite remarkable.

There were also the warrior pastors Andrew and Beth, who assisted me in one of the greatest battles of my life—the parasitic attack on my body. When I met them, I had no idea this battle was even on its way. Andrew and Beth prayed and stood with me every single day until I was healed. This team of warriors was assigned to me when I was fighting for my life. Warriors Elian and Alan helped me through the unconventional treatments to help me heal. The education delivered to me just by this life and death encounter allows me to help others win health battles too.

I will never forget meeting the spiritual mentors who helped me win the battle of forgiveness, allowing me to walk in love and teaching me that I didn't have to be a victim. Michael and Rena were some serious warriors. I will never forget Michael and Rena and all the love they poured into the women who became some of the greatest leaders in my organization. During Michael's battle with cancer, we had a night just for him in celebration of all that he had contributed to others. Rena and I had many fearless conversations, and I shared with her my darkest secrets.

One of those secrets haunted me until the moment I shared it with Rena. You see, when I was a little girl, I prayed that God would take me away from my father—my chicken coop—or take my life. Very boldly, she said to me: "Did you ever think that just maybe He answered your prayer when your father disowned you?" I had never even *considered* this as a possibility! But it was the truth. If I had never been disowned, I believe the death sentence of being a victim the rest of my life would have choked the life out of me and my pursuit of magnificence.

This couple mentored Peter and me in so many ways and played an intricate role in our spiritual maturity and understanding of God's love. The gift of Michael and Rena was invaluable to the contribution of who I am today. I believe that all these great teachers along the way prepared me to encounter the warrior magnificent who had the most significant impact in transforming my life forever. Of course that was my beautiful mentor Marilyn.

I had met many warriors leading to that point, but I had never met a warrior magnificent like Marilyn. She was a multi-millionaire who would never make one dime off the investment she poured into me. This woman taught me how to *truly* pursue the magnificent and inspired me to follow my vision with an *unapologetic, fierce, unwavering* passion. She had an addiction to helping other people win. This woman helped me fall in love with myself so I could help others fall in love with their own magnificence. The great warriors under my own leadership have risen to their magnificence all because of this warrior eagle who walked beside me and taught me all that I needed to soar.

All the mentors in my life have contributed to the person I am today and will be in the future. Those great warriors are invaluable in my life, and there is no way I could ever repay them for all that they have given me or even taken away from me in the pursuit of the MAGNIFICENT.

Their mentorship was with me in the Dominican Republic while I was helping impoverished children with an organization known as Compassion. I had the opportunity there to help so many little warriors. Remember my walk on the beach when I told God: "I want to *feed* the children—not just with food, but with love. I don't *ever* want a child or anyone to ever feel unloved." I asked God to give me an opportunity to use my story to help these children and anyone else who feels unloved or less than magnificent. The opportunity presented itself because my mind and my heart requested it. That is the reason I was in the Dominican visiting all the young little warriors.

I will never forget when I sat down with all the young moms. Instantly, I knew why I had won those battles—it was for this very encounter. I told these precious young warriors that they had nothing to fear and that God is the father to the fatherless. I said, "Do you see that big guy over there—my son Nathan? It seems like just yesterday he and my daughter Amber were on my lap. I was so very frightened just like you are feeling." I assured them that they are fearfully and *magnificently* made, and I promised them a victory over their battles. I invited them to just stand by me. You know, the look in their eyes was familiar. I knew that they were 100% confident that this warrior magnificent would help them soar! We will have victory over this battle so you can help others win too.

I have been accused of being "addicted to the win," and that is a very accurate analysis of my passion. I am surrounded daily by women who are hungry for the invitation to "stand by me." The invitations go out daily from my office, and I could never get tired of pouring love and belief into these young warriors. Why not? Because I was BORN to infuse the magnificence into leaders. I have the honor and gift of mentoring my three children as well as my beautiful daughter-in-law Virginia. I also have a precious little grandson named Isaac who is in training to be a warrior. Peter, as always, is the ROCK and wind beneath the wings of this warrior eagle magnificent family.

The organization I have built over the last 21 years consists of thousands who are hungry for the magnificent. This also inspired my two sons to build their businesses in the middle of a recession. Why? Because they want to make a contribution beyond the "me, me, me plan." Don't ever ignore the magnificent—pursue it mightily with all of your heart and mind. Anyone can just "survive" in the chicken coop of life; but to make the decision to truly pursue the magnificent and follow your vision with an unapologetic, fierce, unwavering passion—that is to be admired. An addiction to helping other people win isn't an insult. It's a legacy worth passing on.

You have now officially been delivered your invitation to stand by me. The question is will you stand no matter what and pursue your magnificence so others can be encouraged to soar beyond anything they could have imagined—all because you accepted this very rare invitation? Remember that it's *your* life, *your* magnificence, and more importantly, it's *your* legacy to pass on. There are warriors like me praying for you to enter their life so they can breathe belief and love into you, helping you to find the courage to win. There is a Cinderella out there praying for her fairy godmother to show up and assist in her transformation to the princess that was there all along in her heart and mind. Don't ever dress down your magnificence. Paint yourself with the most vibrant, brilliant colors of that somewhere over the rainbow.

Stand or Sit? Wimp or WARRIOR?

Your life. Your choice.

YOUR MAGNIFICENCE.

IT'S ALWAYS ABOUT OTHERS

Only real warriors will take the time to read through this book in its entirety. Wimps are just constantly craving to be entertained instead of really reflecting on what it is we are destined to be creating and then living not for ourselves but for others. For those warriors who want the truth (because you know it is required to fulfill the calling of the warrior), here is some powerful truth for those who mentor others and/or have the passion to be mentored by an *uncommon* mentor.

MENTORS AND PROTÉGÉ
– BY MIKE MURDOCK

Recognition of an Uncommon Mentor

Wisdom determines the success of your life. There are two ways to receive wisdom: mistakes and mentors.

Mentors are the difference between poverty and prosperity; decrease and increase; lost and gain; pain and pleasure; deterioration and restoration.

FACTS YOU SHOULD KNOW ABOUT AN UNCOMMON MENTOR:

1. An uncommon mentor is the master key to the success of a protégé.
2. An uncommon mentor transfers wisdom through relationship.

3. An uncommon mentor guarantees promotion.
4. An uncommon mentor can determine your wealth.
5. An uncommon mentor can paralyze your enemies.
6. An uncommon mentor can cause influential people to listen to you.
7. An uncommon mentor will require your pursuit. He does not need to know what you know; you need to know what he knows.
8. An uncommon mentor is more interested in your success than your affliction. His focus is not the celebration of you but the correction of you.
9. An uncommon mentor is not necessarily your best friend. Your mentor loves you too much to leave you the way you are.

> Best friends are comfortable with your past. Your mentor is comfortable with your future. Best friends ignore your weaknesses, and a warrior mentor removes your weakness. Best friends are cheerleaders, and the mentor is your coach. Your best friend sees what you do right, and your mentor sees what you do wrong.

10. An uncommon mentor sees things you can't see. He sees weaknesses in you before you experience them. He sees an enemy before you discern him. He has already experienced the pain of a problem you are about to create.
11. An uncommon mentor will fight against philosophy, pitfalls, or prejudices that would rob his protégé of experiencing complete success in life.

12. An uncommon mentor can create an uncommon protégé. Everything you know will come through mentorship, by experience or a person. Invest everything to spend time and moments with an uncommon mentor.

UNCOMMON PROTÉGÉ WILL HONOR THE MENTOR

1. The uncommon protégé will invest everything to stay in the presence of the mentor.
2. They uncommon protégé follows the counsel of the uncommon mentor.
3. The uncommon protégé reveals the secrets and dreams of his heart with the mentor.
4. The uncommon protégé freely discusses his mistakes and pain with the mentor.
5. The uncommon protégé defines clearly his expectations to the mentor.
6. The uncommon protégé gladly sows seeds of appreciation back in to the life of a mentor.
7. The uncommon protégé ultimately receives the mantle he serves. Transference is not a fantasy.
8. The uncommon protégé moves toward the shelter of the mentor during hard seasons. During hard times, the protégé should pursue the mentor.
9. The uncommon protégé will change his own schedule to invest time in the presence of the mentor.[/NL]

The uncommon protégé is someone who discerns, respects, and pursues the answers God has stored in the mentor for their life.

If you were given one million dollars, how would that change your life? A leader driven by purpose deeper than his own personal needs would only become more passionate about helping others. In fact, this is always the driving purpose of magnificent warriors. They have an uncontrollable desire to help others succeed. A leader who would allow the comfort of money to create an apathetic leadership style, which is all about managing rather than leading by example and helping others win, should really take a moment and reflect on this statement: God doesn't elevate us to keep us comfortable; he wants us to replicate leadership in others.

The gift of mentoring is the ultimate honor. Leadership is a responsibility, and the bottom line is that the privilege to serve as a leader should never be about us—it is always about others, no matter how much success or money it manifests in our own personal lives. If a leader can't be responsible with a team of five, then it is delusional to think they are capable of leading a team of one hundred or one million. Leadership is always about the daily example we live, whether we have millions or we have pennies. Never complain about the demands of leadership; it is a gift!

I absolutely love observing champions because I absolutely, positively know that they will give 100% no matter what. Champions don't entertain excuses or find creative ways to put off their goals. In fact, they understand the value of the moment. Champions don't believe in obtaining it tomorrow, because their minds are set on today—right now—not later. Champions are obsessed with winning and improving themselves every single day. They innately know that the win is not only for them; but more importantly, the win is there to inspire others to win. That is the real force driving the champion. Sound familiar?

Warriors learn to operate in their strengths and celebrate their gifts instead of obsessing about their weaknesses. The truth is we all have weaknesses, but the champions have learned to spend the majority of their time operating in their strengths and a very small portion of time improving their weaknesses. We never want to compare ourselves to others because we usually compare our weakness to their strengths. Instead, we must CELEBRATE our strengths because that is where our victory lies.

Let's think about it ... God-given potential will never inspire a soul if we choose to stand still. To all the champions out there who have allowed your spirit to be stirred: remember the only decisions you should be making right now are decisions to move your dream forward—right here and right now! Operate from a place of joy and confidence because you are born for magnificence. You are royalty; and if you are there in your mind, you will hit your goal—just keep going!

UNSTOPPABLE

Could you get excited about creating a life without limits? Do you have a desire to exceed the limits of what status quo thinks is possible? Just how extravagant do you dare or even allow yourself to dream? The root of the word "extravagant" means to exceed the limits, and it will be an unstoppable mindset that will let you set yourself apart from the herd mentality of the status quo and make the desires of your heart a reality. As a young single mom, I chose to master this unstoppable mindset—and yes, it is a choice.

> *"Ultimately nobody can ever make your choices for you. Your choices are yours alone. They are as much a part of you as every single breath you will take every moment of your life."*

At one point in my life, I actually tried to convince myself that because of certain situations, people should cut me a little more slack. But you know what? I was actually trying to lie to myself. I was giving myself an excuse. If we desire to live in the magnificent, we must confront these lies and excuses. There are people who have had it worse than you or me, yet they never allowed life to stop them because they know that when you are unstoppable, nothing can hold you back. The stand-up warrior has mastered the unstoppable mindset, and it is this characteristic that will propel you into the unstoppable and release the extravagant that exceeds the limits of our logical minds.

When I tell you I was broke, I am not talking about a little broke. Rather, I was flat-out broke. I was penniless, busted, and disgusted with myself, and I was ready to confront the lies that were affirming average results in my life and that were agreeing with the very fear I was ingesting daily from my environment. I thank God every single day that the government paid for my college education as well as gave me the short-term support I needed to get on my feet. But you know what? There was just no way I wanted to stay there. Being on government funding is part of a survival mentality, which is polar opposite of an "unstoppable" mindset that propels us to live out our dreams.

If you study history at all, you can see that we have allowed legalism, prejudice, religion, politics—you name it—to dictate who wins and who is destined to lose. No human on earth should be given this power because they didn't breathe life into our existence. God did. So, I figure if God created me, then I would have to conclude that He has a huge say in my destination if I refuse to fall prey to the limits imposed by society. We have the power to choose so we can back down or rise up—to be stopped or to be unstoppable.

Every day, I see people obsessed with keeping up with status-quo thinking. So many talented, brilliant warriors have lost themselves to it, and I just want to see *you* break through these limits and move into the unstoppable. I am sharing all of my junk with you so maybe somewhere deep down inside you can actually accept the truth that YOU are magnificent too, and nobody can keep you from this but you. The only reason I am not a statistic is merely because of the daily choices I made to be disciplined—to be unstoppable. Every situation in our lives is only temporary because anything is subject to change. It doesn't matter if you are in a pit. What matters is that you do something about it here and now.

I know what it's like to just get by and constantly worry about paying the bills. I didn't find it very empowering to constantly worry and feel desperate every single day, having to rob Peter to pay Paul and having creditors constantly calling me—not to mention banks refusing to even give me a *checking account* because it was that bad. I made a *choice* to do whatever I had to in order to change my life. I made a CHOICE to not accept government funding as the answer for the future. It was just a temporary solution that would propel me to something better, and I made a choice to only be there for about one year of my life.

Having to stand in the grocery line to find I didn't have enough money for everything I needed, and having to put food back was a pit kind of moment. Having my power turned off in the middle of winter, putting blankets up, using a kerosene lamp to warm the room, and telling my kids that we were pretending were pit moments. Though, in actuality, I think we were really pretending at that point because in my mind, that situation was temporary. Our situation was subject to change because that reality was NOT going to be my children's future or mine—because I had made the choice that it wouldn't.

I remember working three or four jobs—whatever it took to get off public aid and move in a forward, unstoppable motion. It is a choice to succeed or fail, and it is a choice to operate in faith or fear. Faith and fear can't operate together; so if you are going to take your life to a new level and operate in the unstoppable, you have to be a warrior of great faith and declare war on your fears. You know the fear I'm talking about—the fear that can hold you back. This fear says things like, "What if you follow what is deep in your heart and you fail? What if the people around you don't support you? What if your walking away from the herd makes people upset? What if they reject you? What if you run out of money? What if you end up moving away from the familiar and you don't know what to do?"

Seriously, you know the things we see as stop signs. Everyone has them—fear, rejection, friends, family, low self-esteem, money, children. I could go on all day long and fill up an entire book, or we can be truthful and bold enough to call out these things for what they are: excuses and dressed-up lies that we tell ourselves to deflect what we know deep down inside. We can be unstoppable as long as we declare war on fear and doubt and all the things that we let stop us.

We could find the unstoppable courage in pursuit of the very thing we are created to be and fulfill. You can ignore the stirring inside you that wants more and continue to find yourself living a life full of limits, or, you can have faith—choose to be unstoppable—and experience the limitless mindset only rewarded to the few who make that choice.

STOP SIGN: REJECTION

Let's look at the questions that come from fear, and let's propose some of those same questions in a positive light. What if the people around you, the ones who are supposed to be part of your future, DO support you? What if the people who don't celebrate you finally leave so you can move forward with your dream? Have you ever heard "Go where your cause is celebrated not tolerated"? That, my friend, is some very wise advice. What if your walking away from the herd actually reveals to you the truth: you didn't belong with the whiners and complainers of this world anyway. You should be partnered with the unstoppable dreamers that actually DO make things happen. Pursuit of the dream will bring joy into your life and those around you, whereas staying with the herd is only motivated by fear. And fear leads to nowhere.

Who really cares if people reject you? The truth is that everyone is not going to like you, and that is okay. They don't have to like you for you to walk in your magnificence. Let's rewind my story and talk just for a bit about rejection. If I can overcome being disowned by my family, then you can handle rejection from people who are not celebrating your magnificence. And a true warrior will walk away.

When Peter and I got married, he was insistent that he could fix my family because he just couldn't comprehend how an entire family except one sister could literally turn their backs on a single mom with two kids. He would say to me, "There is never a good enough reason for any mom or dad to abandon their daughter and grandchildren." He wanted to push through my parent's whole insane stance on disowning their daughter and grandchildren, so he suggested that we should attend my niece's wedding because my mom and sisters and other family would be there.

You see, Peter is from a very loving Greek family, and he just couldn't comprehend that anyone could actually display so much hate toward family. Even though I had already been disowned for 18 years at that point, he had to see this for himself. He wanted to prove that he had done everything to fix it. I see so many people trying to fix others; but the truth is simple … we can't. Only God can change someone's heart.

As a side note, putting yourself in situations of abuse is not the answer to reaching any kind of positive result in your life— no matter who it is that is inflicting the pain. A person should never be labeled or treated as worthless, and no one has the power to label us worthless unless we grant them permission. God created everyone with a purpose, and that purpose is to be magnificent in the unique gifts and possibilities that He put in us. We must make the choice to never let someone make us believe or see differently.

Well, I went along with Peter's plan. He finally convinced me to once again put myself and Sam, who was four at the time, into that environment just one last time. After 18 years of our existences not being acknowledged, it was pretty obvious to me what would happen, but we went anyway—though it was with great hesitation.

I had already expressed to Peter my concerns about the possible rejection and shared with him my cautiousness of exposing Sam to this. After all, Amber and Nathan experienced the ultimate rejection from these very same people at an early age, and I didn't want to put Sam in their space. Sammy, of course, had never seen my parents or any family members except one of my sisters, so he was full of unconditional love for them. He sat by the window in my office drawing picture after picture for my mom. Sammy has never had any grandparents because Peter's parents passed away years before. This was the only so-called "Grandmother" he would ever have.

I will never forget him running over to me with his beautiful pictures in hand, with a huge smile on his precious little face and a light in his eyes that would penetrate anyone's heart and soul. He said, "Mommy, I know when my grandma sees these pictures she will love them and love me too!"

Can you even imagine this? I could see history repeating itself all over again. It was just like the day when Amber and Nathan wanted so badly to be accepted by the very family who were absolutely great with pretending we did not exist. In that moment, the tears started pouring out of my eyes. The way Sammy loved at that moment is *exactly* how we should all love—a completely perfect love that continues to give, even if the people around them are abusive. The lessons of love are demonstrated so beautifully and perfectly through the eyes of a child.

As a child, I remember doing the same thing. I thought if I just could fix *me,* then maybe my parents would love me like I desired to be loved. Your family may have never abandoned you; but in today's world, it is so obvious that people are starving to be loved and crying out to feel affirmed. The desire that Sam had for me and my mom to love his pictures is the desire every human being on earth has: we want to be loved! It doesn't matter what we pretend on the outside. Inside, we just want people to celebrate our "pictures." We never know the pain someone is feeling deep inside that propels them to paint these pictures, so it's not our place to judge. That day, when Sam handed me what he drew, I looked at him and said, "Of course she loves you, Sammy. And she will love these pictures!"

My heart was saddened—not for Sammy, because he would always be showered with love. I was saddened for my parents and family because they had missed out on Amber's and Nathan's beautiful gifts. And then they decided to reject Sam as well, which was a huge loss for them. Peter insisted that we take Sam to the wedding, so I listened because I thought maybe things could change and after 18 years— maybe Peter was right. I thought maybe we could put this behind us once and for all.

The wedding ended up serving as a final closure for me. This experience was honestly a necessary event to end this painful chapter of my life. Through this experience, the man who loved me deeply and unconditionally was able to confirm in me that these people indeed—family or not—are full of hate, not love, and that we deserved so much more. Peter told me that he had never seen anything so inhumane in all of his life, and he has experienced some very deep pain himself.

When I arrived, the tension was high because no one thought we would actually attend. However, because of my rock of a husband, I decided to be unstoppable and go. My father and brothers didn't show up to the wedding. I guess it's not a shock because then they would've had to finally face me after 18 years—and I'm sure that was just something they weren't going to face. I walked into the room where Annie was getting ready and embraced her with a big hug. I told her she was absolutely beautiful, and all of a sudden my mom walked in.

I had a choice to run away or proceed with the unstoppable and walk toward her. I chose to walk right up to her, and I hugged her without hesitation. I told her I loved her and that she looked beautiful. With that, she left the room without saying a word. That day, I stood for love and refused to allow all the hate and rejection that was thrown at me to destroy my spirit. In the end, I embraced the attitude that no matter what, I had to tell myself, "Jamie, just love her." I think that's why it is so easy for me to love all the naysayers in this world. It doesn't really get much worse than your parents and family disowning you and your children. Anyone else after that is seriously no big deal.

After attending the ceremony, we went to the reception. We were placed in the back of the room away from all of my biological family. My sister put my mom, my other sisters, and the grandkids at a table with her. Peter, Sam, Amber, Nathan, and I were put in the back. This was the last straw with Peter because we were literally treated like worthless trash. My husband said that before we left, he was going to meet my mom and introduce her to Sam.

I said, "That's not a good idea, Peter."

His reply was, "We are going to speak to her."

I will never forget this moment of ultimate rejection—not just of me, but of my baby boy Sammy. Peter went up to my mom and said, "Hello. I am Jamie's husband Peter, and this is your grandson Sam."

My mother looked down at Sam with the most cold-hearted glance—like he was the most worthless piece of junk in the world—and said, "Hello." Nothing else. No hug. No response. No, "You are my grandson! So nice to meet you!" There was *nothing* other than an ice-cold glance that left me and my husband speechless and chilled to the core. And then my mom walked off. We left the wedding, and I cried the whole way home.

I didn't cry for myself—it wasn't me that she rejected. I was used to that. I cried that this evil hate was now inflicted on my four-year-old son, just like it had been on Amber and Nathan at the very same age. Why am I telling you this story? To teach you this lesson: *Don't repeat lessons in life because you believe you have the power to change someone.* We only have the ability to transform ourselves, and we can pray and hope that in time our love may be a message to help those who spew hate to others and that in time, they will catch on.

If I can overcome this kind of hate in my life and turn it into something magnificent, I promise that you can too. However, it will require that you walk away and stop allowing others to make you a victim. They don't want to remove the cancer from their hearts. We can't be responsible for other people's choices if we want to move forward with the unstoppable. We can push through the fear of rejection and become better people in the process. A warrior can, and a warrior will.

To this day, Sam still remembers and talks about that day. When he got in the car, the confusion he felt went away fast. His dad and I smothered him with love and chose not to focus on the negative. For our family, this was the final closure and we chose to never expose our kids and the beautiful family God has blessed us with to the hate that had been continually inflicted on us for so many years. We decided to finally let go and let God handle it. There is something really wonderful about being able to let go, and it's a very important ingredient to the unstoppable.

It is also imperative that no matter what happens and who rejects you, or how scary it might seem to leave the familiar, you must keep moving forward in life toward the people who celebrate you. We can't move into our future if we keep holding onto the past and the hate. After all, the people from our past are not necessarily supposed to be part of our future. It's great if they want to come along and celebrate with you; however, if they insist on injecting pain into your life without any remorse, don't grant them permission to take this ride. And yes, you DO have a choice! Forgive your enemies and choose to love them, but please walk away after that. If you don't, you will be paralyzed and they will prevent you from attaining the very magnificence you are destined achieve.

If people can walk away from you, reject you, and consider you worthless, then it is time to let them go and stop allowing history to repeat itself. It's time to *change* your history because they are not meant to be part of your future. Get excited about the new people who are waiting to celebrate you in this unstoppable movement toward the magnificent. Even in the face of rejection and ultimate hate, you must master the unstoppable and move forward, or you will cave in when the naysayers hate (which they will). I wish that I could tell you they won't, but the truth is that there will always be haters and naysayers on the journey. You just need to be able to let it go.

So now let's look at the questions I asked at the beginning of the chapter differently: "How will I feel when I meet all the people who are going to embrace me and my ideas? And how can we work together to create something that will exceed beyond the average—something of great extravagance and limitlessness? How will it feel when I can help others overcome their fear of rejection and be inspired to LIVE instead of just survive?" Time isn't going to slow down for anyone; and believe me—when you overcome the fear of rejection, you will become unstoppable.

I remember when Sammy was little, maybe two years old, and we were eating lunch at Cracker Barrel. Sammy saw a bunch of these stuffed animals that he loved in a big barrel. He would pick one up and just hug it. Then, he'd pick up another and hug it too, then another and another. It was simply precious. A child about eight years old came over to where Sam was and looked at the animals. This inspired Sammy to pick out his favorite and offer this sweet gesture to this eight-year-old boy. But the response wasn't *"Thank you."* It was *"Let's ignore you."*

Most of us would either take offense or think *"Who cares?"* and cop an attitude. But children don't see life tainted like that. In fact, Sam just picked up another stuffed animal and offered that one because his desire to bring this little boy joy overruled the rejection that was being inflicted on him. Needless to say, the boy walked off. That didn't faze Sam because pretty soon a little girl walked up and was ready and willing to receive Sam's precious sentiment with a smile that lit up the room. She gave Sam a huge hug that blessed them both.

The little boy did not celebrate Sam; however, the little girl did. That's just life. If a two-year-old can be rejected by a boy after simply offering him a stuffed animal, why would anyone think that we will ever be the exception in life and never experience this? If you want to be unstoppable, you must keep asking and giving until you find the person who was destined to receive your gift and just let go of the ones who aren't ready to celebrate your magnificent. In building a business, you have to be willing to ask and ask again, just like Sammy did, until you meet the leaders who are destined to be part of your dream.

In the movie *Finding Nemo,* Dory tells the little fish Nemo to just keep swimming. This is *exactly* what we must do: just keep swimming. Even if there are people along the way that just don't get it, just smile and walk in love and keep swimming. You will absolutely get to where you have imagined yourself to be.

> *"Whenever you are confronted with an*
> *opponent, conquer him with love."*
> *– Mahatma Gandhi*

STOP SIGN: MONEY AND TIME

Let's move on to another stop sign that no one wants to confront or really speak about very much: MONEY. We can continue to put our heads in the sand and pretend that living paycheck to paycheck is a really grand plan; however, you didn't pick up this book for that, did you? I strongly believe that we can live a life of abundance in all areas of our life, which will pour over into others. When we get past the just-pay-the-bills mentality and make enough to not obsess about our bills, then we can actually get on with the real show—what we are born for, our magnificence, our contribution to others, how we will service humanity. I wasn't picky about the occupation I had, as long as I could pay the bills. I just knew it was part of the process that had to be completed to move forward to the real deal.

I absolutely refuse to believe the gifts we are given are supposed to be ignored because we have to get a job we don't like simply to survive. So many people get to the end of their life and have regrets of "I wish I had done this or that." Every single human being on this earth has some kind of legacy—a special contribution to offer the world—and it is beyond working a passionless job to just pay the bills.

You see, we can't operate in our magnificence when we are obsessing about paying the bills. We have to get to a point in our lives that our contribution will extend outside our own household paycheck and bless those around us. I took my life from receiving public aid to building a multimillion-dollar business. I think the insight I can share might help those warriors out there who are still hesitant to pursue their dreams because they fear losing money.

I hear a lot about the fear of not having money, and this is my response to that little stop sign (or should I say BIG stop sign): If you want to create an unstoppable mindset, you must stop worrying about money. Oh, I know this definitely goes against the herd mentality and logical thinking of this world; however, have you ever noticed that people who always worry about money never have money? And people who don't worry about money somehow always seem to manifest it? Even when I was on public aid, I always found a way to make more money even if it meant working more jobs. I knew there was plenty of it out there; it just required one magic word—work—and the unstoppable mindset to move life forward.

I was never too good to turn down an opportunity to work because I knew it would help my children have a better life. In today's world, there are so many people who just think that they are owed success and money. In my business, there are thousands under my leadership, and very few show the discipline to pursue the unstoppable. There has been a delusional mindset infused into society that tells people if we ignore our money problems long enough, they will go away. But guess what? They will only get worse unless we pursue our dreams with passion and face the truth that we can pay now and play later or we can play now and pay later. Either way, the paying will happen.

In creating my business, I was required to *give,* even when I didn't have the money to. It's not a big deal to give when you *have* extra. The real test is believing enough when you are struggling financially that you SOW into a dream anyway and summon the faith to get to the harvest. You can and should find ways to make more money, but you must also have faith enough to invest what little you have and know it will grow.

The warrior doesn't plant just a few little seeds in the field to get a harvest, nor does he worry about the field even when the unpredictable elements of life come his way. He just *knows* that the seed will produce a harvest when he plants. Can you imagine a warrior going out to the field and worrying, wondering, or crying over the seed until it grows? Sounds a little crazy, right? I would put money down that some of you have put a seed (money, time, etc.) out into the field; but because you didn't see something instantly, you started to worry. Maybe you even cried over it, and you decided to quit before you ever gave it a chance to grow!

You will *never* see an unstoppable warrior stare at the seed he or she has sown and cry or go into the field after a few days and pull it out of the ground because it hasn't grown yet. I see this all the time! The problem is that people are looking to get rich instead of being passionate about pursuing their purpose. There is an enormous difference in these two types of planting, and they bring totally different results. Planting a seed to just get rich is all about the ME, ME, ME plan. Everything is focused on your personal satisfaction in the moment.

The seed we put down in the unstoppable pursuit of our purpose for others, however, will last way past our lifetime. It will harvest a legacy.

There is always a risk involved when we walk away from the average status quo of society; however, in my experience of building a very successful business, it always requires that we sow time and money. If you are afraid to talk about money, invest money, or sow money, then you will be stuck living within the limits of status-quo thinking. Again, this is *your* life, *your* choice.

Investing time is straight-up a must to succeed as well. Without it, we can forget any possibility of manifesting magnificence. People often think that they can create a life without limits while operating in the mindset of an employee, but it doesn't work like that. Your request is to exceed the limits of average—you are requesting the *extravagant!* You are asking to live past the limits of status quo so you can ultimately attain freedom and opportunities that will never be available to those who don't take the risk and stay inside the limits. To do that, you cannot be average or put in an average effort.

I encounter numerous people pretending to plant their seed by being busy but not productive. They're just wasting valuable time because while they have deep desire to reap a harvest, they don't want to spend the necessary time and effort needed to achieve their vision. We are a walking bag of seeds, and pretending to plant is quite different from the actual discipline of planting that is required to produce a real harvest. A real harvest takes time and effort. The truth about sowing is that we must first invest the money to buy the seed. Then we need to spend the time putting it in the ground and nurturing it daily. The ground is most fertile and green where we sow and consistently nurture daily. So remember: daily discipline and the right choices bring the unstoppable.

You absolutely can't stop the warrior who has a compelling vision they have faith in. So my advice to you is to sow into something that you believe in and are willing to go to work for. Action is the proof that we truly have FAITH in the seed we have planted. All my questions about whether a warrior will succeed and break through limits can be answered by simply observing where the warriors invest their time and money. It is obvious by their choices if they will quit before the finish line or if they will complete the race by what intent they have for planting seeds, the time they put into it, and what actions they prioritize.

It really comes down to your priorities. When you are serious about the unstoppable, your entire life will be evidence that you mean what you say because of the choices you make daily. For instance, the friends you hang around, the books you read, where you invest your money, and the time you spend pursuing your dream—or maybe the procrastination in your life that has continually delayed your dream—these all show your priorities. Warriors who pursue the unstoppable will spend every available minute obsessing over their magnificence. And believe me, you don't find them perched in front of the TV watching ridiculous reality shows that will *never* bring them to a new level in their life.

When I left corporate America, pursued my dream of owning my own business, and unleashed the entrepreneur in me, I put down money and time. When I wasn't working my job in this transformational stage of my life, I was in pursuit of the freedom I desired for my life and my children. You would have never caught me wasting hours in front of the TV or doing things that did not serve my family or propel me toward my goal. I was the perfect student because I was willing to do whatever the expert entrepreneur instructed me. I was just that UNSTOPPABLE in my mind because I was more than ready to get out of the limited, little-box of a life I had created by following the status quo. Do you want to get out of your little box? Then be willing to put a payment down on your dreams just like you would if you wanted to take ownership of the home you have dreamed of.

Warriors have a desire to contribute their time and money to something significant that will actually inspire others. We must continually ask ourselves whether or not our messages will lift people to a new level of their lives. The time we invest helping others discover their greatest potential is a priceless gift. For me personally, it was a gift given to me so graciously by my mentor Marilyn 21 years ago. The gift of belief and love could have only been infused into my life by the TIME and MONEY she invested in me without wanting anything in return except to see me succeed. My friend, *that* is MAGNIFICENCE.

TIME is the most valuable asset we have in life, and we can't get it back! When we sow time, it should be invested in what we consider to be our priorities in life—our visions that will help others. You tell me how in the world watching TV is actually going to contribute to something extravagant that empowers us to exceed the limits! When I flip through the channels on TV, which is NOT often at all, I see the most ridiculous programs. I just have to turn it off because so much of it is just the ME, ME, ME plan out there. "Hey look at me. I'm a bad girl or a wicked wife! Maybe you can be desperate like me!" I am sure this will infuriate some of the people who produce these programs, but it's the truth.

My daughter lives in LA, and she tells me that the majority of America watches these reality shows that require no talent and very little money to produce. These kinds of shows have put the *true artists* out of work. There are seriously some extremely talented, creative people who have a powerful message to deliver; and if you are one of those warriors who has a passion to really create and perform, my advice is to pursue the MAGNIFICENT and don't settle for the get-rich plan, as it offers nothing of significance to others. Sure, you might make some quick money—maybe even get rich—but in the long run, is it really significant and fulfilling to your legacy? Or is it just about a ME, ME, ME program sold to Americans every single waking hour of the day?

SOWING A LTITLE SEED

You must have a team to build a dream, and that dream will fail with a mindset of fear. A warrior doesn't entertain doubt and fear because they are constantly on the battlefield willing to pursue a cause that contributes to others.

Their team clearly exemplifies this attitude as well, so a real warrior attracts leaders who are willing to put time and money down and join a vision that is greater than their little box of small thinking. The team we have around us is absolutely a reflection of our belief in where we are going. A warrior's compelling vision and pursuit of the magnificent attracts the right team, and these leaders have something deeper going on than just paying the bills. This kind of team understands that living outside the little box is where a warrior feels the most alive and thrives. A warrior is born to win the battles, born to help others, and born to contribute on a deeper level than just the household needs.

The constant movement of enlisting other warriors on our team is imperative because there will be fall-out in pursuit of the unstoppable. If you hesitate in enlisting people to the team because you got your feelings hurt before, then the outcome will be LIMITS. So keep moving forward. I assure you that there are warriors praying for you to invest time and money and tons of belief into them so they can bust out of their box and live a life without limits. You will never have a problem finding the quitters in the world because they are everywhere.

If I want to win a battle in life, the last mindset I want to enlist is the quitter. If you want to win, you don't just line up all the quitters and ask their expert advice of "What do you think?" You go to the WARRIOR—the winners in life—and ask them. Ask someone who has won the battle you are in at this very moment. I can assure you that this warrior will help you summon the qualities you must have to be unstoppable. Remember that *this is your life, your choice, your dream. Dream and live* or *doubt and die.*

As you know, I have two very successful sons who are also entrepreneurs, and it has been such a tremendous blessing watching them pursue the magnificent. I can assure you that they both had to sow a lot of seeds to reap a harvest and build viable businesses that they continue to do daily. One night when Sam was probably 12 years old, we were playing *Monopoly* out on the lanai. He was learning a lot about sowing from his brother, as this was around the time that Nathan started his own business. Sam could hear the conversations between Nathan and me about him investing in his dream and all the doubters who offered their expert advice that Nathan should get a "real job" with that business degree. [Remember: don't ever take advice from someone who has never done what you are about to do. Let them be a cheerleader, but don't listen to their advice because they have absolutely ZERO idea what you are going through.]

So Sammy was absorbing vital information from these conversations about being an entrepreneur. He was like a little sponge—more than any of us could have even imagined. We were in the middle of the *Monopoly* game, and Sam was losing really badly. He started to give money away and letting people land on his property and not pay rent for it! He would just say, "Sowing a little seed, Mom. Sowing a little seed."

Ironically, he actually made the greatest comeback that night and won the game! It was just like the many times I have experienced this in my own life and observed the warriors around me who give to others and always reap a harvest that they can't contain. Actually, it's pretty awesome how this works. The key, however, is that you can't put the seed down with any doubt. If you sow with doubt, then just forget it. Fear and doubt are brothers, and they don't mix well with faith and belief. In fact, they are arch-enemies. So just keep this in mind: you must believe. Faith is believing in what can't be seen in the natural. Remember: it is in our mind *first,* and it requires a compelling, unstoppable vision.

We have to get out of the little-box, small thinking and push ourselves over the line, past the limits, and this requires that we sow with faith, especially when it is uncomfortable because that is when it matters the MOST.

Let me warn you of a little red flag in enlisting the right team and a finding a warrior. Sometimes, I hear someone say, "I don't need any money. I'm comfortable, Jamie." That's how I know that they are selfish. They are, in fact, showing ZERO desire to do anything else other than help themselves. All I heard was the ME, ME, ME plan. The

most successful warriors in the world, who make a lot of
money, could just sit back and do absolutely nothing, but
they are all about winning battles. The unstoppable mindset
is passionate about helping those who can't pay their bills.
The most selfish thing anyone could ever do is tell me, "Oh,
I don't need anything. I'm comfortable." Then can't you help
someone else attain something?

In my business, I have seen women in their 70s who retired
at $30,000-$70,000 dollars *a month*, yet they still pursue
passionately their love for helping people live in their magnificence. Clearly, these warriors are not helping people because
the warriors NEED money. They are pretty comfortable. The
truth is I don't need money either, but I definitely want to
make a whole lot of money because it will allow me to be able
to help a tremendous number of people. Whether you want to
talk about this or not, money is influence. People do not listen
or follow people who are broke. They follow success. Warriors
want to influence the masses with a positive message. I tell
people all the time, "Hey, if you have plenty of money, can I
send you the countless e-mails that I get daily of people who
actually need your money? Because clearly you have missed the
whole reason God blesses us with money in the first place."

I know this is blunt, but it drives me *crazy* when I see
people who have a lot of money be self-absorbed over insignificant things or, on the flip side, when I see capable men and
women refuse to work harder to make a difference in other
people's lives.

I was just speaking with a wonderful man today named
James, who is the security guard in my neighborhood. He was

telling me why he loves what he does. This man, who is probably at least 75 years old, is a security guard not because he needs money, but because he wants to influence the kids in the neighborhood in a positive way. If James was worried about his bills, the last thing on his mind at 75 would be speaking to the children. But because he has more than enough money, he can put himself in an environment daily to make a difference in the lives of people in our neighborhood.

I love people like James because the conversations are always coming from a place of love. It's funny that just a few days ago, I had the exact opposite encounter with a woman who was extremely wealthy. She, too, was probably at least 75 years old, and she was unhappy. In fact, I would describe her as mean. It was obvious to me that she needed something to do with her money besides get her nails and hair done while talking to the people who served her like they were worthless! There are a lot of people who are in positions of wealth who haven't done anything significant with their wealth except serve themselves.

I know it will really upset people to hear this, but somebody has to tell the truth! I still can't comprehend how there can be homes worth *millions* of dollars that sit just blocks away from children going to bed hungry every single night. It is just *tragic!* The warriors must serve until they die. No matter how much wealth they acquire, warriors will continue to help people until they take their last breath because they have a clear, UNSTOPPABLE comprehension that we are here to contribute to a greater purpose beyond ourselves.

LIVING YOUR MAGNIFICENCE

I would like to share with you a beautiful example of someone who lived out her magnificence until the day she passed away—my warrior magnificent mentor, Marilyn Welle. About two years ago, I called her and asked if she would come to speak to my leaders about their magnificence and just share some great life lessons and wisdom. It was a very sad season in Marilyn's life because her daughter had just passed away from cancer. She was starting to sound despondent when I would speak to her on the phone. I felt compelled to put a reminder in her heart and mind of just how significant her love and belief had been and continued to be for me and countless others. I reminded her of all the women's lives she had changed by being a fearless warrior and passing her belief on to others. The seed she had sown over the years was impossible to measure because it will go on for many lifetimes.

You know those feelings you get deep down that you need to move on something *now*? Well, a warrior listens to this prompting because there is always a reason for this stirring. How many times have we said to ourselves, "*Oh I probably should think about it. Maybe the time isn't right.*" A lot of people thought my timing wasn't right to ask her. But you know what? They weren't warriors. I knew it was time to get her back in the battle. Deep down I had a feeling that this would be the last time my leaders would have the opportunity to learn from this master, so it was something that was unstoppable.

Marilyn hadn't done a public speaking event in quite a few years, so at first, she was quite reluctant. But I expressed to her how much her love and belief in me had created such a tremendous legacy, and I wanted my leaders to meet the woman who had started it all. Marilyn's love and belief in me created a legacy in my life that all the money in the world could never afford because my gratitude is endless. You see, it goes back to that sowing thing—the unstoppable farmer. Well that is what "sowing" pure love and belief will produce—a legacy that never fades.

We flew to Las Vegas where Marilyn lived and held a conference so that one hundred of my best leaders could sit at the feet of a warrior magnificent. It is always an amazing thing to sit at the feet of magnificence, don't you think? I would have never, ever missed a minute that this woman offered to speak to me. In fact, I would have dropped anything at any time if she had something to say. Marilyn's advice trumped the advice around me because she was where I was going—and she was in fact *the expert.*

Marilyn busted out of her little box. Even with being married to an alcoholic and being the mother of six children, she never gave up on the dream that she was indeed a master of the unstoppable. I knew when I heard her voice over the phone, without even meeting her in person, that she had the key to my destiny. I could feel it deep down inside that she was the teacher who would change my life forever. And guess what—she did!

Many people never experience this in their lifetime because they don't want to let go of the familiar people and move toward the future because they are just not open. The warrior is the student who is praying for a teacher who will summon the excellence from them and teach them how to win. When you are a warrior, you will do *anything* to get in the space and glean from a master warrior. You know that it's all about gaining insight and wisdom so you can grow and continue to learn. We hope that a mentor can cut the learning curve down for the inexperienced warriors.

As I said before, NEVER, EVER follow a mentor or a leader who is in neutral because they can't infuse you with any fresh revelation in the pursuit of your dream. You can tell when someone is in neutral because the information they put out is the same—with zero passion or relevance for today. Their advice is totally boring and ineffective in moving forward, and it is evident that they are no longer going to battle for anyone.

Mentors worth listening to are the ones who are still out there, even at 70 plus years old, and are passionate about investing their time and wisdom into others. Marilyn was that kind of warrior.

Over one hundred of my leaders followed me to Vegas. These young warriors had clearly demonstrated a desire to lead and were willing to invest their time and money so they could glean from this warrior magnificent. Peter and I got there the day before so we could spend time with Marilyn, and we met at the hotel for dinner. When we arrived, Marilyn was at the slot machine waiting for us. That was typical of her because she loved to play the slot machines. I hadn't seen her in over a year because of my parasite dis-ease, so it was so great to see her. It was as if no time had passed at all. Isn't that funny? When a person is truly destined to be in your life, the time you may have spent away seems so short. When you are in their presence, it seems as if it was just yesterday. It was like that with Marilyn and me.

We went to dinner, and Marilyn shared with me in depth about the loss of her daughter to cancer. She shared that she had been in a deep depression over it because this was the most devastating moment in her life. My heart sank because I had never heard her talk like this in the 20 years I had known her. Marilyn looked me in the eyes while she held my hands and said, "Jamie, thank you for reminding me that I have something to live for. I know that I lost a daughter, but you are also my daughter. I love you just like I loved her."

In that moment, I was sure glad I didn't listen to all the little-box people who couldn't believe that I would even *request* time with her. This amazing warrior shared with me that she was actually nervous about speaking again, but that she was forever grateful. She couldn't stop thanking me for asking her to speak again because it had brought her out of a very dark depression. True warriors can become depressed when they stop using theirs gifts to help others because they are BORN to help others WIN.

The next day, Peter and I walked her into the room with all these young warriors who she had impacted beyond anything that she could ever even imagine—except she didn't even know them! They knew her through the legacy she had passed down through me. Every leader in the room stood in awe and clapped for her, that courageous warrior magnificent. Just her presence brought tears to the eyes of these young warriors because she didn't have to say a word; you could feel the magnificence all over her. It's funny that a warrior never really has to say a word because their strength and countenance is so powerful. You can feel the *fierceness* in them, yet you can still sense a gentle and loving spirit.

It is quite a gift to be in the presence of a WARRIOR MAGNIFICENT, so you really better pay attention when given such an opportunity. I don't see much respect in today's world for the warriors who have gone before us. In fact, I see a lot of disrespect and dishonor because again everyone wants the ME, ME, ME program, but the warrior magnificent will definitely correct you on that. Be forever grateful if God has placed a warrior in your life who believes enough in you to tap you on the shoulder and say, "Come with me. You have what it takes to be magnificent and lead others to win in life."

The two days she shared were priceless, and the stories were coming straight from her heart with ease because she was the *real deal*. Warrior magnificents don't need a single note because they are going to just speak TRUTH straight from their heart. They speak from an overflow of experience. Many of my leaders said that they cried when Marilyn and I walked in together. They could feel the love and respect that I had for her and she had for me.

There is nothing more powerful than walking beside a warrior magnificent. It is an unstoppable movement because there is a supernatural strength in a relationship with a true mentor. I'm not talking about the cheerleader mentor with the pom-poms in hand who enjoys cheering you on but has never won the unstoppable battle. Believe me—there are many counterfeits out there pretending to be a warrior, but they are living vicariously through the real warriors. They didn't have the guts to ever take the risks involved in pursuing the magnificent. I'm talking about the warrior magnificent who has gone to hell and back with you, won many battles before you, and then teaches you how to do the same.

I'm talking about the mentor who never gives up on you, even when you are in the pit of your life because the mentor understands that the pit is part of the process of winning. I'm referring to the warrior who knows all of your darkest secrets yet still believes in you, still loves you, and will always take an unwavering, fierce stance for you until you believe your magnificence is truth. I considered it my greatest honor to walk beside Marilyn and was willing to say goodbye to my stop signs just so I could continue to sit at the feet of such a faith giant.

After Marilyn had spoken for two days, my husband Peter was emotional because he was reminded of what this woman had done for our family without wanting anything in return. Peter got up and reminded all the leaders that Marilyn, who was in her seventies and had just suffered the greatest loss in her life, made a decision to come out of retirement because she loved people and still had a passion about making a contribution to our magnificence. Peter's eyes were full of tears as he said it and felt Marilyn's love.

Marilyn was there for one reason only: to pass on wisdom that would help us win our battles and reach our magnificence. That great warrior was there to teach us how to live out the extravagant—a life without limits. Marilyn stood on her feet for hours for two days straight, and I watched her pour and pour and pour because that is just what a warrior will do. Great mentors will pour as long as the students are hungry.

You would have never known that she was retired because her passion to pass something significant on to others was burning brighter than ever. It was the best I had ever heard her speak, and it was such an honor to behold. This faith giant, the real deal, this warrior magnificent—she is the one who I had the honor of serving and learning from for 20 years of my life. It is simply impossible to put a price tag on what she gave me.

And you know what? If I had allowed those stop signs we talked about earlier to infect my mind and prevent me from creating the unstoppable mindset and movement, none of what I have or will ever contribute to others could have ever happened. I owe Marilyn everything I have because she sowed a limitless amount of time and money into this very frightened single mom and made absolutely nothing tangible from my success.

She poured unconditional love and belief into a young woman who felt unworthy of any magnificence, only to see years later the seed that she had planted turn into a harvest of the magnificence that will live beyond her lifetime. I say all the time that Marilyn and her love for me has been one of the greatest gifts in my life, and she was a complete stranger I met at the age of 27. You see what happens when you meet the mentors of your life. Just because I let go of the familiar and sowed my time and money, I was blessed with a warrior magnificent. I am so glad that I called her and asked her to do that conference. It was the last time she spoke before passing away from cancer only one year later.

I often think back on those two days that Marilyn stood for *hours* at the age of 72, probably pushing through a whole lot of pain, just to pass on all of her magnificent wisdom to an elite group of young warriors. Leaders like Marilyn are true warriors whose message has contributed to the "helping others win" program, not the ME, ME, ME microwave idea of success that is so prevalent in our world today.

I remember after she was finished pouring all that she had at the conference, we walked out, and she said to Peter and me, "I always feel so protected and loved when I am with the two of you." That is exactly how I have felt since the day I heard her voice over the phone and knew she held the key to my magnificence. With her, I was sheltered, protected, safe, and very much loved. Marilyn sowed daily without fail and taught me to do the same. Now, I have passed this on to countless lives. Marilyn, just like all great warriors, had a clear understanding that sowing our time and money in other people is needed to operate in the magnificent, and it was a great honor to glean that from true excellence.

The TRUTH ... it is really no big deal to sow money when there is plenty, or sow time when you have time available on the calendar. We have to be willing to sow when it is inconvenient and really uncomfortable if we want to create the unstoppable movement that brings us in to a life that exceeds status-quo limits. I have to check my motives daily in leading other leaders because if we are operating out of love for people and what is best for them, the actions we take will be unstoppable in helping them bring out their greatest potential.

The saddest part of society is that as a whole, we seem inoculated to the pain going on around us and just assume that it is somebody else's responsibility when, in fact, it is our role as a society to help. I see healthy, capable, intelligent people refuse to work and make a contribution because they think they are too good to serve at a level that may seem "beneath them." They don't understand that serving is the greatest honor there is. We pride ourselves in our great education, but who is educating people on serving? I don't care what degree you have or how much money is in your bank account. If we don't serve and love people, we have absolutely NOTHING of true value—nothing that will live past our lifetime. How many people are able to bring their things with them when they die? No one. If we refuse to serve and not show an interest in others—an interest in encouraging them to WIN and feel valued—then we are living a very shallow existence that will end sadly. There will be nothing of real significance that will be passed to others from us.

People have it backwards. When we contribute to others, we will see our lives change for the better; and when we help others succeed, we will see ourselves blessed beyond measure. The greatest among us will choose to serve; and when you are a warrior magnificent, you will be compelled to lay your life on the line for others. I think the misconception in leadership today is that we think we should be served more the higher we go. However, the more influence and voice we have been given the privilege to have, the more humble we should be and more willing to serve others.

The narcissistic attitude celebrated in our society honestly makes me sick to my stomach. While people are dying all around us, kids are being sold into sex trafficking, women are being abused daily, and poverty is increasing all over the world—we continue to take in daily infusions of selfishness.

As the human race spews hate at each other, the noise of "What about ME?" continues to get louder and louder. People gain outrageous, self-righteous attitudes because we have actually appointed ourselves the big JUDGE over society. In reality, that is an illusion because not one of us has ever breathed life into a human being. We are not God.

If we want to exceed our limits, we must walk in love and be a positive vessel for others instead of wondering how something can help us. We have 70-plus-year-old men and women living in poverty, and they are bagging groceries at the stores for the 20-to-50-year-olds. We have young, capable adults who are too lazy, think they are too educated, or think it is beneath them to serve because they are too busy feeling important. I rarely see people around me actually embrace the word "serve."

And yet we can have nothing of magnificence without serving. I am a firm believer in creating wealth and living a prosperous life; but to me, it begins and ends with being the ultimate servant. We are blessed to be a blessing; and in the end, those who contribute only to the ME, ME, ME plan will end up lonely and afraid with no legacy.

It is so sad that people actually think they are connected because of all the technology out there, but the truth is that people are so disconnected from actual passion that they don't contribute into the lives of others. Personally, the delusional mindset that tells us we are entitled to success just because we have a degree is why the subject of money is so very sensitive to address. The truth is you have to get off the ME plan and focus on the plan of helping to contribute to others, which will absolutely involve truth and an unstoppable, forever-servant's heart. That plan requires that we pay now, not play now, so that others who have no ability to help themselves can benefit. I am not referring to the people who are irresponsible and refuse to work. If you are healthy and capable of working, then do whatever it takes to move yourself forward no matter what opportunity is presented. I'm referring to those who can't work because they truly need help from those of us who can, and we must help here and now.

You will be amazed how fast your life can change in a positive direction when your focus on others. My advice to you is this: If you suffer from depression, poverty, sickness, divorce, death, loneliness, etc., then go and SOW into people and make a difference in their lives. I promise you that your life will be transformed dramatically.

When I was a single mom, the hardest time for me was the holidays. I hesitated to share this next small portion of my story; but after I really reflected on it, I was prompted to share because I think the story demonstrates a HUGE part of how I know helping others is the only way to access the magnificent.

To some people, my story is super traumatic; but to others, it's no big deal because they experienced deep pain in some other way and also summoned the warrior inside of them.

These great warriors were not willing to lose the battle of their life. I'm sure most of you reading this could never imagine yourself with no family at all during the holiday because it is a time that brings great hope and love around the world. Many people consider it the perfect opportunity to put differences behind them and move forward as we move into another new year. I can tell you that the holidays were a very lonely, dark time for me before I married Peter.

No family ever invited me to holiday get-togethers. However, my children had grandparents on my ex-husband's side of the family, and I just really felt like it was best for them to visit there so they could experience the love of grandparents that they could not get from my parents. So, every holiday I would dread the moment when I would hug their sweet little necks and send them on their way. Of course, we always celebrated with our own tree and presents, just the three of us, prior to Christmas Eve.

I would pretend to be so glad they were going to their grandparent's because I knew this situation was just temporary, and the last thing I wanted them to feel was any sadness that I would be alone. I did a pretty good job with this until they got older. Every year, like clockwork, Thanksgiving and Christmas would come. I knew my children could feel that something was terribly wrong deep down because they eventually came to realize the truth of what had been happening for those 12 years. I always insisted that they went, even though the selfish part of me wanted to hang on tight.

Many times during those holidays, I really wanted to just die because the pain was so deep and the rejection was so harsh, but all I needed was a reminder of my children and their

MAGNIFICENCE to stir up my own magnificence and to find a way to push through.

Now here's the irony of the whole story: remember the sister I mentioned that had not completely disowned me? Well, my sister was married to my ex-husband's brother, and what that meant was she was with my children and my ex-husband's family during the holidays while I was alone. I'm still not sure why she or my ex-husband's family never invited me to their meal. I was just a couple of hours away, but I suppose they had some really great reasons behind their decision, right?

At any time, I could have refused to let them go; but because I cared more about my kids then anything, I chose to walk in love. That is exactly what warriors do. They let go and move forward, still in love. It is easy to love the people in the world we really like, but the greatest evolvement of the human spirit is to walk in love with those who spew hate at you. That is the real test to pass; and believe me, I have definitely passed it after almost 30 years of being disowned.

Let me remind you, however, that doesn't mean you put yourself in their space to be treated unworthy. I don't care what your differences are. The fact that my sister never invited me to dinner, and my children were with them at Thanksgiving and Christmas, was a pain that was honestly indescribable. After all, can't we just be together for even a day for the sake of my children and their well-being? I guess the big question for me was how they could love my children and treat me, their mother, with such hate and rejection.

I know there are many people in the world who walk around in denial, and I really believe that in my situation, there were many things done in denial. The truth is that they probably still are. After Sammy was born, knowing that he was Amber and Nathan's brother, my ex-husband's family sent zero invites for Sammy. This, of course, was something that made Sammy feel confused. After all, the rest of the year Amber and Nathan were with us every day. We were an inseparable family except when Nathan and Amber went down to be with their dad, his family, and my sister.

This has always been a strange situation because this sister does not acknowledge Sammy's existence, only Amber and Nathan's. I mean, there are times where she is forced to face it, like at my son's wedding, but the knowledge is then put back into the denial box of life. A very loud message is sent out that Amber and Nathan are separate from Sammy, Peter, and me, which is just bizarre, right? The truth is when people don't want to face the real truth, they will live in denial. I was forced to face the truth head-on because it was *me* who was disowned and cast aside. Do you know that the people who are being challenged with painful situations like the above must RISE up and face the truth that they and only they can change it by their choice to live, not die? It doesn't matter if everyone else is in denial because everyone else isn't the person who is dealing with the painful situation. The truth is people can't really understand your pain unless they themselves have experienced something similar.

In most cases, people walk around, turning their head away from the people around them who are crying out for help and love every single day. It is called total denial because they are too afraid to *see* the truth. It's not just my sister who has done this. It is literally the majority of the herd who walks around oblivious to other people in pain. My greatest gift in the world came out of these very dark moments. I had to face them and summon the faith and courage to actually make choices that would assist me in moving forward, not backward.

Focusing on your pain will never help anyone—not others and not yourself. We can't focus on the "symptoms." We must be intent on the solution and the purpose of why we are here and what lessons we can learn from this. There has to be a great lesson behind our pain. The deeper the wounds we have in life, the more we can be used to help others if we are willing to put down the victim mentality and inspire others with the WIN of the WARRIOR. I personally believe the reason I am so fiercely passionate and compelled to help others is because of the pain I have overcome and pushed through in my life. All warriors have conquered great pain. I assure you that my story is not the only one out there, and neither is yours.

Focus on the win. My war scars are a reminder to me that I can help others through the battle because I actually got to the other side, and they can too. I think the saddest thing we encounter along the way in pursuit of the unstoppable is that not everyone wants to be helped. It is difficult to watch people who insist on living in their little box, but we must let them go.

In the long run, it was in those darkest moments of my life that I summoned the answer to such pain. I told myself, "Jamie, find some people who need you, who are lonely and might feel abandoned and rejected like you." Do something with your pain. Turn it into something magnificent! The remedy that helped me push through to the unstoppable was no longer thinking about myself and blessing others.

So every holiday or moment I came face to face with this pain, I focused immediately on others. As a single mom, I would work any shift I could find during the holidays or any day when I knew that I could sow some kind word or hear someone's life story. Do you know what I discovered? There were a whole lot of lonely, rejected people who were also feeling some very deep pain. The stories I could tell you of elderly women and men who were forgotten because their kids were too busy to visit. I could tell you stories of orphans who were elated that anyone would even teach them how to apply makeup or read them a cool book about Santa Claus. There were shelters I would visit with frightened women who did not know what tomorrow was going to bring but were comforted by me. I had inspired them to get up and fight one more day and helped them realize that they and their children are of great value and worth winning the battle for. That's the deal. We need people who do more giving in life than waiting around for someone else to do it.

I remember the teenage girls who had run away from home pregnant, feeling rejected and labeled by everyone. I knew exactly how to encourage them because I had already won that battle. One night, I was working as a respiratory therapist on one of those 12 holidays, and the doctors approached me and asked me if I would go speak to this pregnant teenage girl. I remember walking in her room. All the lights were out because she did not want any light in her room at all. At first when I went up to her, she would not speak to me; but because I understood her pain, I was determined to sit with her and talk even if it took all night. This little girl needed to know that someone like her got to the other side. It was after I shared my story—from one very young mom to a soon-to-be one—that she grabbed my hand so tight and looked me straight in the eyes with a very piercing glance that reminded me of the times when I had also been so frightened. She asked, "Do you promise it's going to be okay?"

I said, "ABSOLUTELY, yes! It's going to be better than okay, and that's because you were born for something really extraordinary. Don't you ever forget that or let anyone tell you any different." It was shortly after our warrior-to-warrior talk that the lights came on in the hospital room, and the curtains opened up to let the sunlight in. She made the choice to get up and fight.

I could fill up an entire book on those 12 years of holidays when I put myself in a position to serve. Even now, I will continue to contribute to others' lives because I am so passionate about encouraging them to pursue the magnificent. Any of us could get really comfortable and choose to turn our head away. We can easily choose to be in denial about our surroundings and how many people need love and encouragement, but I refuse to be that person. I am clear on what brought me out of the pit and into the palace, and I will continue to get this message out because it literally saved my life. I have seen it transform others as well. The more hope, love, and faith we sow into others, the more that will come back to us. Pretty soon, if you do this, you will find yourself in a place that is UNSTOPPABLE and absolutely exceed all of your expectations.

I have a really great story on being a servant to others, and I know you will love it! My husband Peter was able to retire from a job he hated when Sammy was two, and this gave him the opportunity to play an active role in our son's life. Peter had an ardent desire to be there every step of Sam's life as Sam grew up. Peter coached Sammy in football since he was four years old; and at the age of eleven, we made the decision to sign Sam up for a football league here in Florida called the Bull Dogs because of Sam's passion to play tackle football. My husband went to the league and asked if there was any possible way for him to help coach these kids because he played football his entire life and had played on the University of Illinois' team, which is a top-ten university. Now keep in mind, Peter had coached Sam for seven years straight, but now he had to be accepted as part of the Bull Dogs. The politics there were ridiculous. The coach told Peter in a demeaning manner that Peter could be the water boy, but he could never coach because there was no place for him.

I am sure the coach thought Peter would decline. My husband had a choice to make. He could humble himself and serve as the water boy because his desire to be on the field with Sam was most important, or he could let his ego get in the way and watch from afar. Peter agreed to serve as the water boy. He chose to serve no matter what his title was.

I remember going to the games and practices and watching my husband be treated with so much disrespect by these coaches. Even in the face of the coaches' arrogance,

Peter just smiled and served every single day just so he could be near our son on the field. Every day, Peter would bring home around 25 water bottles and dirty towels, and we would wash them for the next day. This continued for the entire season. I can tell you there were hateful remarks by some of these coaches because they were trying to humiliate Peter off the field. However, Peter was unstoppable and just kept moving forward, rising high and walking in love.

At the end of the season, the coach—who had been hot-tempered, hateful, and just honestly one of the most arrogant people I have ever met—got in a fight with a *woman* on the field, causing a riot to break out. As a result, this coach was terminated from the league. It is true that we reap what we sow in life, and the next season, my husband was on the field coaching our son until Sam went on to play in high school. If my husband had not SERVED as the water boy and paid the price to contribute to Sam's dreams of football, who knows if Sam would have developed the confidence he has today.

So we have sure covered a lot about the unstoppable, haven't we? I think we can all agree that without a servant's heart for people, there will never be a promotion or an accomplishment worth a whole heck of a lot outside of the self. You have heard me share that even in the hardest moments of my life, I made the choice to serve. Though that period was one of the most painful times in my life, you can see it also held, and will continue to hold, some of my greatest moments.

The warrior magnificent will continue to ask this question daily: "Who can I help get to the other side and WIN their battle?" The truth is that true success is summed up in a word that very few people want to pursue. However, it is the ultimate quality required in a warrior magnificent—and that word is "serve."

THE MAGIC IN MAGNIFICENCE

Today and for the last 16 years of my life, our holidays are filled with all of my children together as one family. Every year, we go to Disney World, which is my FAVORITE destination on earth besides the beach. The memories we have created over the last 16 years are priceless, and they will continue to be just as amazing in the future. Disney is one of the most MAGICAL places on earth to me; and maybe when I bring my family there, it gives me an opportunity to bring back the things that were put on hold in my life. I love every single magical moment it has to offer humanity in all its extravagance. We can all agree it definitely exceeds the limits of what anyone thought could be possible—at least everyone but Walt Disney.

Can you even imagine what he must have come up against when he expressed his VISION to the herd? I am sure if you have read anything about this brilliant warrior, you can see that it was indeed an unstoppable fight for the magnificent! He told banks that he was going to build a magical, extravagant park and base it on two mice. Let me ask you, why is his VISION any more significant than yours or mine? The truth is that it's not. The difference is that he chose the UNSTOPPABLE.

He didn't enlist the quitters, the people with negative attitudes. He set out to find a team who would be passionate in helping him create this magical, unstoppable, absolutely EXTRAVAGANT DREAM! And one he could share with the world.

When our family first arrives at Disney, the energy is out of control because the child inside of all of us has literally been unleashed the minute we drive onto the grounds. The extravagant environment gives us power to connect on a new level of dreaming and allows the unstoppable vision for our lives to be unleashed in a magical way. I totally believe in this because when you play, you can create. When you put yourself around the extravagant, you will attract the magical. When we arrive at our hotel, the staff immediately says, "Welcome home" and "Have a magical day." How can you not smile when people say to you, "Have a magical day"? To me, home should always be so magical!

Have you ever thought to yourself, *"Do my actions encourage people to have a magical day?"* This magical place inspires people to get on buses, sing songs, and act goofy, and it is absolutely contagious. The magic of joy and love is everywhere at Disney World, and it doesn't get better than that! In fact, we can only hope we could spread as much joy and love.

You will discover two very different groups of people at Disney World. One is the family who are so caught up in the lines being long and things not happening fast enough and whatever else is going wrong that they can't enjoy this magical experience. I always feel bad for those families because they never pause to just appreciate the beauty and detail that has gone into this extravagant masterpiece. They want to complain and focus on the negative instead. The truth is that these kinds of people will never be happy because if they can't get happy at Disney World, then they don't have much of a chance elsewhere. I don't know what to tell them. In my business, I see leaders like this. They want to fixate on all of the things they see wrong with the picture—the things they don't like about building their dream.

The other type of people you will observe at Disney and in life are the ones who will do whatever it takes to make the magical be more magical; and just by their very presence, they will inspire immediate forward movement, high energy, and excitement. Warriors bring more energy to places and have a deep appreciation for places like Disney World because they understand the discipline, commitment, and creative talent that is called upon to create such an extravagant, magical kingdom.

So when you see these two very polar opposite creatures at Disney World and in the pursuit of your dream, you want to be very selective and intentional in making connections with joyful men and women who allow themselves to embrace the childlike spirit that is inside all of us.

Here's some truth: "When you wish upon a star, your dreams really can come true. With just a little bit of belief and some pixy dust, anything is possible when you believe!"

Creativity, dreaming, and connecting with the childlike faith in every person is necessary to bring what may seem impossible into the extravagant. It's all in how we communicate our message and whether we are willing to connect with the people who are supposed to be in our future. I remember one trip to Disney, Sammy was about four, and we were going from the Magical Kingdom to the Wilderness Lodge where we were staying.

There was a boat to take us across the lake; and when we got to the line, they shut the gate. We thought we would have to wait longer, which could have been a disaster because Sammy was very tired. Anyway, we didn't get upset about it, and pretty soon, they actually came back and let us on the boat as long as we were fine sitting on the floor. We got on the boat, and all of us got on the floor, which was totally perfect because we were just glad to be on the boat, right? Have you ever felt like that—you were just glad to get on the boat? You made your goal by an inch, but wow, it felt great even though you were on the floor.

Anyway, while I am sitting there, this beautiful little girl, who looked about six years old, kept staring at me. Her entire family was all speaking Spanish, and I had no clue what they were saying, so I just kept smiling back at her. Pretty soon, she got up out of her seat, came over to me, took my hand, and motioned for me to come sit by her as she made room for me and Sammy. She was just the sweetest little girl, and she literally lit up the entire boat with her smile.

Sammy had a glow light with Mickey Mouse on it, and he was just waving it back and forth. He then offered it to her. She just smiled while they passed it back and forth without saying a single word. The little girl would point to something, Sammy would do the same, and this went on the entire way back. I could see her thinking really hard about how she could communicate or connect with us if she didn't know English and we didn't know Spanish. I could feel her thinking about this because honestly, I wanted to break the language barrier too. All of a sudden, she started to sing, "I got the JOY, JOY, JOY down in my heart." Sammy sat up with a HUGE smile on his face. He said, "I know that song!" Then, they both started singing it together.

Once the boat stopped, we got off, and all three of us hugged. The lesson she taught me has stayed with me since that moment. The truth is that this little girl did everything she could to break through a language barrier in order to connect to us because she was compelled to love people. I often tell the groups I speak to that if everyone in the world would put this much effort in connecting with each other, the world would be vastly different.

The lessons we learn from watching children are absolutely priceless because it brings us back to the truth and beauty of the childlike spirit that lives in all of us. That is why we must persist in protecting our hearts from things that can taint or pervert the beauty of wishing on a star—the purest form of belief, joy, hope, and love—which will bring an unstoppable extravagant movement. I could tell you so many stories about Disney and the holidays spent there, but the thing I want you to see is the DREAM NEVER DIES. Dreams still go on because of a warrior's UNSTOPPABLE pursuit of the magnificent.

We can transform our life and inspire others when we declare war on average, status-quo thinking and embrace the magnificent. Our family of seven is growing even as I write my first book because love is unstoppable. Our home in the future will be overflowing with more grandchildren and family who will bear witness to the extravagant picture I created in my mind from the very beginning when I was just a single mom who made my wish on many stars and a choice to fight for the unstoppable. The magnificence and love filling our lives is evidence of my belief and action, and I know this party is just getting started. *Dream and live*—that is the ONLY way to do this thing!

I am forever grateful that the behavior of others did not paralyze me for all those years and that I turned my pain into a deep, profound purpose. If we can just keep in mind that we are not fighting people, we might be part of another's process to confront his or her own demons so that person can also move toward the magnificent.

The behavior directed toward us is never about us and what we did or didn't do—right or wrong. Hate and anger come from something that needs healing inside of other people. We all have the choice to allow this hate in our life or to let it go and let God do the fixing. I think for me, I always remind myself that when people hurt me, it's because they are in so much pain, and all we can do is refuse to accept the insults, rejection, labels, or hate thrown out and just walk in love. Warriors always RISE above negativity because if they don't, it will stop any movement toward the extravagant, magical, magnificent future they have created in their mind.

My decision since I was a teenage mom to pay now and play later has always served to be the right one. I was willing to pay any price in my life to make a significant contribution to my children, and now I see this influence expanding in ways that I could have never imagined possible. But that was part of the choice I made to NEVER give up and continue to pursue the magnificent.

The unstoppable mindset will ask the questions: "Who can I help next?" "Who can I serve?" "What problem can I solve?" In my business, the question I ask myself daily is, "Who can I encourage or empower to get up and WIN the battle to walk in their magnificence?" and "Who can I share my story with and encourage to know that they can do anything they believe is possible?" There are people who may respond to me with hate, but then I ask myself this question: "Is this person responding to me hatefully because she doesn't like me, or is it really because she is hurting?" Hurting people hurt people, just like the little boy who was hateful to Sam in the Cracker Barrel. I have always said, "Ugly on the inside, you are butt ugly on the outside, and I don't care how much money you have, what car you drive, or how well you dress— you can get all the plastic surgery in the world, but the inside of a person is where it all emerges."

We can't paint the pain because eventually the truth emerges; and when a person is squeezed, you most definitely can see the real deal under pressure. When people are mean to me, I just seriously say a little silent prayer and walk in love because I refuse to focus on anything that comes from fear. Do you know how many people are crying out for the ultimate servant, the warrior magnificent, the people we have an opportunity to make connections with every single day just like that precious little girl in Disney? What about the single moms like me who are waiting for their Marilyn to pour belief and love into their very spirit so endlessly and to help summon the warrior inside of them? We must be unstoppable and SPEAK LIFE into others and see them as MAGNIFICENT, not agree with what society has labeled them to be because they don't fit into the little box.

We must demonstrate with our own example that living in a poverty mindset is something we have the power to change. I believe if we are concerned about running out of money, we will never live past the limits that money can impose on people who make that the dominant thought in their mind. Money is the most elusive thing there is. When I had no money and the car was being repossessed and creditors were harassing me, I just paid whatever I could little by little and focused on what I could do that would lead me to living past the limits of just getting by.

The more you give, the more will come back to you. So if we are more afraid of losing money than investing in our dreams and in others, then our life will be limited. We can't manifest the magnificent when we partner with any type of fear—the fear of rejection, of losing money, or something else. It most definitely will keep us imprisoned with self-imposed limits.

When I lost my corporate job and began to pursue the business opportunity that led me to a limitless lifestyle today, I had to remove my greatest fear FIRST. I remember calling up my friend and asking her, "If I fall on my face and don't make this work, can I live in your basement?" That may sound really simple to you, and it was because I had already been on public aid and promoted myself to corporate America; so to me, it was that simple.

The thing about the unstoppable warriors is that they have already conquered their fears on many levels, so they are equipped to do this again and again. People who protect themselves in life and refuse to be stretched can be devastated by life when it happens, which it always does. But the warrior is more interested in living life, not just surviving it. Warriors are unstoppable because they refuse to lose, and they will make lemonade out of any lemons handed to them by life. You see, I had to declare war on FEAR in order to move forward; and as soon as I knew my children would have a roof over their head if it was needed, then I was ready for the unstoppable because we would make it no matter what. I am so glad that the fear of money didn't prevent me from pursuing my dreams.

I was saying no to headhunters who wanted to hire me, and they told me how very ignorant I was to not take the job. I just *knew* this was the opportunity that would lead me to a limitless lifestyle. I think you can agree it was definitely worth it to me to get "SOULED" out on the magnificent and create the unstoppable mindset required to exceed limits.

You have to make a decision to step out and refuse to operate in or entertain fear. People talk about fear being okay, but you will never convince me of this because I believe that fear paralyzes us from attaining the magnificent. It requires faith in something to see it manifest, and fear is the opposite of faith. How is it that so many people want to infuse fear into their everyday thoughts? Again, it is a choice, and a little bit of fear is like taking a little bit of poison. Eventually, it will destroy anything faith and love can create. God didn't give us the spirit of fear; He gave us a spirit of courage and love.

Personally I choose to believe this truth. I know some
people will disagree or analyze that, but you are reading this
book because you want to know how a disowned single mom
of two went from the pit to the palace, and this is part of the
formula I have lived by my entire journey. Keep in mind that
what you choose to criticize and disprove you can never have
because you don't believe it. So it's *your choice, your life.*
Dream and live or *doubt and die.* Personally for me, I chose to
pursue my DREAM and master the unstoppable mindset that
is ever-present in every warrior. Remember this book is not for
the wimps; it is designed for the warrior. I made a decision to
fight back from the choices I made that led me to the pit, and
I asked myself this question: "Jamie, what is your 'why'?" The
answer was (and still is) my kids, which was the magnificent
that I was reminded of every single time I looked in their eyes.
What is your" why"? Is it something you can't put down no
matter how much you try? Because that's what it needs to be.

A "why"—a purpose—is required to be unstoppable. In
fact, you must become obsessed with the why and willing to do
whatever it takes to create it. Being unstoppable will require
the RADICAL, so again ask yourself. Did you really pick this
book up for your ears to be tickled, or are you really ready
to see transformation in your life? Because let me warn you,
the status quo will tell you all the things to fear, what can't be
done, and why you should play it safe. Don't listen to them.
Listen to the warrior magnificent.

The warrior magnificent will passionately infuse you with
the belief that you can do whatever you visualize. The warrior
magnificent will say, "Go for it. It's now or never. You are born

for magnificence." Which voice do you choose to listen to? Do you want fear or fearless, extravagant or pennilessness?

The "why," the compelling vision in people's heart and mind, is their ENTIRE CORE and will actually be the very thing that ignites them to contribute into someone else's unstoppable mindset. If you are brave enough, bold enough, fearless enough, and are willing to invest and serve enough in this unstoppable movement into the magnificent, you will bless those people who may not have the strength to fight right now and are literally praying for the warrior magnificent. Remember that you win to help others win.

Think back to the last time you allowed yourself to Wish upon a star. More importantly, when was the last time you DECLARED WAR on all the challenges that have kept you from pursuing the very reason you were given the gift of life in the first place? Get up and fight. Get up and WIN! Stop feeling sorry for yourself and go love on those people who are in more pain than you. I promise you this: through that, every single limit that has ever been imposed on you will be broken into little pieces.

WHAT IS YOUR MASTERPIECE WORTH?

About five years ago, I read a story that truly impacted me and the way I think about love. I would like to share it with you. A wealthy man and his son loved to collect rare works of art. They had many priceless pieces in their collection from artists like Picasso and Raphael. When the Vietnam conflict broke out, the son went off to war. He was very courageous and died in battle while rescuing another soldier. The father was notified and grieved deeply for his only son. About a month later, just before Christmas, there was a knock at the father's door. A young man stood at the door with a large package in his hands. He said, "Sir, you don't know me, but I am the soldier who your son gave his life for. He saved many lives that day. He was carrying me to safety when a bullet struck him in the heart, and he died instantly. He often talked about you and your love for art. I know this isn't much, and I'm not a very good artist, but I think your son would have wanted you to have this."

The father opened the package and found a portrait of his son, painted by this young man whose life was spared. The father stared in awe at the painting, and his eyes welled up with tears. The father thanked the young man and offered to pay him for the painting. "Oh, no, sir. I could never repay what your son did for me. It's a gift." The father proudly hung the portrait over the mantle. Every time visitors came to his home, he took them to see the portrait of his son before he showed them any of the other great masterpieces he had collected.

The wealthy man died just a few months later, and there was an auction for his paintings. Many influential people were there and were excited at the opportunity to purchase some of these great works of art. As the auction began, the painting of the son sat on the platform. The auctioneer began, "Who will bid for this picture?"

There was a long silence until a voice in the back shouted, "We want to see some famous paintings! Skip this one!"

But the auctioneer persisted, "Who will take the son?"

Another voice shouted out, "We didn't come here to see this painting. We came to see the Picassos and the Rembrandts! Get on with the REAL bids!"

But still the auctioneer continued, "The son—the son— who will take the son?"

Finally a voice came from the very back of the room. It was the longtime gardener of the wealthy man and his son. "I will give you one hundred for the painting." Being a poor man, it was all he could afford.

"Give it to him for a hundred!" shouted the crowd.

The auctioneer pounded the gavel, "Going once, twice, sold for one hundred dollars."

Another voice shouted out, "Now let's get on with the real collection!"

However, in that moment, the auctioneer laid down his gavel and said, "I am sorry, but the auction is over."

A voice shouted "What about the paintings?"

The auctioneer replied, "When I was called to conduct this auction, I was told of a secret stipulation in the will that I was not allowed to reveal until this time. Only the painting of the son was to be auctioned. Whoever bought the painting was to inherit the entire estate, including the famous paintings. The man who chose the son was to get everything."

When I first heard this story, I was reminded of all the people in the world who have literally given all they have to a vision that God has placed in the very core of their heart and soul. The dreamer understands the message of the portrait because every dreamer, at one point in their journey, must decide if they are willing to give it all, even when the naysayers consider it worthless. You see, all warriors understand that the value of our dream has everything to do with how we see it—not how others see it. I had to make the decision to give it *all* to the dream God placed in my heart. To experience your magnificence, so do you. To the crowd, one hundred dollars was insignificant. But to the gardener, it was all he had to give. Are we giving all that we have or just part of it? Without *really* throwing your heart over the line and playing 100%, full-out, you can never experience the magnificent.

Can you imagine the faith it took for this gardener to give so selflessly out of love for his boss? You see, the warrior and the gardener have something powerful in common. The gardener took a stand for the wealthy man and his son in front of that crowd. As warriors, we must take a stand for our dreams, no matter how insignificant it may seem to those around us. The world's critics can be screaming for you that you shouldn't be working toward your dream—that it's not as valuable as the other dreams in the world. But that's not the truth. The crowd may not see the dream on your heart as a masterpiece; but as long as you believe it is, give your dream your all, and take a stand, then you will see and live your magnificence.

We must be passionate enough to stand up for what we believe in. By doing so, our contribution to the world can live beyond anything tangible, beyond the material world, and it will be capable of penetrating the very heart of mankind. That contribution is love—straight-up love.

The gardener's decision to love is similar to what every warrior is confronted with daily—can we love enough to serve others while wanting *nothing* in return? After all, that is the ultimate key to magnificence. Do we have *that* kind of unselfish love for others? A poor man gave up all he owned out of love, never imagining the blessings he would receive. A warrior must pass the test of putting it all on the line for love in order to get to the other side. Are you ready to operate in this kind of mindset? This is a mindset that absolutely requires us to serve selflessly in order to live a life of reward that penetrates deeper than material things and requires that we leave a legacy of love.

This warrior mentality refuses to let us believe our dreams are ordinary or common, but rather extraordinary and an actual masterpiece. What will you stand up for? How much do you believe? Is it enough to give it all you have—right here and now? Because the auction has already started.

I am a mother, wife, friend, and mentor to countless women because I took a stand in my vision. It required passion, commitment, courage, discipline, and some very unpopular decisions. It is this same stand you must take for *your* masterpiece, which will ignite the multiplication factor of leadership. I never wondered how God was going to multiply the loaf of bread for me. I just knew He could.

How will you stand when you put this book down, time goes by, and the hecklers ask you how much your masterpiece is worth? Will you be ready to take your stand? I remember having the desire, as a little girl, to travel the world and make a difference. Yet I went along with the crowd, as people tend to do. But deep down, the dream was always there. Even when I reached the bottom as a single mom with a one- and two-year-old, no parents, and no money, as I wondered how I would pay the bills, the dream of magnificence was still there. To me, it was valuable enough for me to stand up and do something about it.

I made a decision to finish the race, even if that meant limping across the finish line. I decided to believe what God placed in my heart: "I have great plans for you." So, I decided it was time to take my stand. Now it's time for you to take *yours* and finish *your* race. The dreams I had as a little girl to travel the world have been exceeded beyond anything I could have ever imagined. When I look at my passport, with all the stamps from the places that I have been privileged enough to visit, I still stand in awe. If I had given up on my dream, my life would not be what it is today. I've been privileged to travel the world and speak to crowds of people who don't even speak the same language. Yet I get to see them find the courage to pursue the magnificent all because of my decision to stand up.

All warriors know that the decision to stand will require that you work harder than the average person will ever want to. I realized that I would do things, say things, believe things, and imagine things that I never did before and that I must be willing to get uncomfortable. I had to be willing to welcome challenges and obstacles that would serve to make me stronger and better equipped in life. Yes, people laughed in my face, spoke down to me, and told me my dream was worthless. In the beginning, it did upset me. But one day, the realization hit me—the same realization I have been telling you from the beginning: "Who freaking cares what people think about my masterpiece? The value of this dream is totally up to me!"

When in doubt, always do the opposite of the majority!

The deal is this: Man's opinion does not trump the God who created me with a specific destiny in mind. I am *so* glad I reached out to my husband who stood beside me, my mentor Marilyn who never gave up on me, and my children. Heck—my kids were never ashamed of me when we were on welfare, so why would they be concerned about what people would think about the manifestation of my dream? The very people who watched me struggle to feed my kids and never even offered to help out, the naysayers who stood by and absolutely expected me to fail—they were of no concern to me because my stance was just way too strong. I was destined to take a stand, so the dream just burned stronger and stronger with every single beating I took along the way. I see so many people running from the hits that are just part of the game. They give up before they even realize just how strong they really could be.

My 16-year-old son Sam is a running back for his high school football team. I will never forget one of the first games he played as a freshman. It takes a lot of courage as a running back to willingly get on the field with the absolute certainty that everyone wants to take you down. This particular game, the team Sam was playing against looked bigger and stronger. At first, he started to let the appearance and size of the players intimidate him because he thought they were bigger, stronger, and faster. He started to think he may need to be more careful in this game. His dad decided to intervene. Peter told him, "Sam, if you go out on the field with *any* hesitation, you will get hurt in the game. You have to go out there with 100% confidence that you will get the touchdown and that *nobody* can stop you."

Isn't that the truth? If we are going to get on the playing field of our dreams, we are not going out there with hesitation—we are going out there to WIN! That night after the game, Sam told us that the other team was trash-talking him after tackling him. They'd say things like "How'd you like that, number 7?"

You know what Sam's reply was? He said, "I LIKE IT. Let's do it again!" Sam said every single time he took a hit that night; they kept trash-talking him. But every single time, he got stronger and stronger as he replied, "I LIKE IT. Let's do it again!" He said it all the way down the field until he got the touchdown.

Do you really play full-out, 100%? And when you take the "hits" that are most definitely going to come at you, how do you respond? It takes passion and intensity to pursue a dream and realize the masterpiece that only YOU can put value on. You may say, "Wow! This all sounds INTENSE!" You better get a little intense if you want to take ownership of your dreams. In fact, do you know what the word *intense* actually implies? When people tell me I am intense, I take it as a huge compliment and quickly reply, "Thank you very much!" You see, the word *intense* is defined as "showing strong feelings; extreme earnest; very great, passionate, fiery, and zealous." That is a lot more exciting than the opposite, which is apathetic, mild, and dull. Nobody follows dull because dull can't cut through to the very core of what you want to achieve. When leaders *really* want to see transformation, they are not looking for dull—they are ready for some intense.

When you truly take ownership of your masterpiece, you refuse to lose and have zero fear when the hits come because it's all part of getting on the field. After all, this is YOUR DREAM, right? When you really want to reach your magnificence, the voices that shout out that your dream is worthless will only propel you to fight back with more passion and vigor because it is what God has created you to do. You were BORN to be magnificent.

You tell me, did I make the right decision to stand? I think I did. The growth continues, and the dream will never die. Why? Because a true masterpiece worth owning will live past any leader's lifetime. The little girl—"the dreamer" who took a stand—is still standing because the warrior in me refuses

to allow anyone to label my masterpiece as worthless. Your
dream is valued at much more than a paycheck of something
tangible; it is valued with the paychecks of the heart and
a legacy that lives on. My son Nathan always reminds me
"Mom, *if we don't stand up for something in life, we will
fall for anything.*" It is so important as leaders that when we
stand—no matter what we're standing for—we do not waiver
in the face of adversity. The minute you make the decision
to stand, there will be small-minded people who cannot
understand true victory because they were too afraid to take a
stand. They will accept their masterpiece as worthless because
somebody who didn't get it, and honestly wasn't supposed to,
actually talked them out of their dream. Warriors, on the other
hand, refuse to stand down. They will forever stand up no
matter what.

BELIEVE IN THE DREAM

*"A leader with faith and vision goes together
like fire and heat.
You can't separate them without destroying
their very essence."*

When you design your very own home, you first have
a picture in your mind of what you want. Then you
design the plan to build it. The house goes up, brick by brick,
and finally you move in and decorate the home you have been
envisioning the entire time in your mind. The OWNERSHIP,
however, begins with the thought of designing your own home.
That very thought brought action to the design and a commitment to the completion of the house because you knew it was
yours to begin with. That is how you take ownership of your
dream. It is time for you to write your vision down, run your
race, and take a stand to finish this great masterpiece. A leader's courage to stand and fulfill a vision comes from *passion*,
never *position*. In order to make your vision your own, you
must first take ownership of your dream in your mind. What
does it look like?

Remember: The race begins when you believe in your
dream and decide that you will finish what you start—*no
matter what*. Keep in mind that confidence and perseverance

will be rewarded, obedience will be recognized, and shrinking back will be regretted. You must know where you are going, and you must know that this journey requires that you take others along. A great dream can never be reached without a team. If you have a little dream, then a little team is all you require. However, a BIG DREAM demands a big team, and you must help a lot of people along your journey.

Little dream, little team.
BIG dream, BIG team.

We can't succeed at anything until we are willing to take the first step consistently and BEGIN. Beginning is doing the first part of an action, so you must decide on the goal and develop a plan. So many people overcomplicate this process by analyzing everything, when in actuality we should be creating and using our imagination. The formula is simple. When we get focused on how we can be contributing to others, the opportunities and relationships will manifest to make it happen. The truth is when you help others get what *they* want in life, you will find yourself with a masterpiece that is priceless. The value increases with every person you contribute to along the way because, as I've said, the key to a masterpiece of any significance is that it's *never* about us—it's always about someone else. Only through serving others can the spirit of a man or woman be at the highest level of magnificence.

We can't sit around and wonder how our dreams will grow; we have to take action. When lives are changed, your team will grow, allowing your dream to continue to enlarge. What a privilege it is to serve the people around us without expecting anything in return! There is a piece inside of us that just knows, "I am BORN to be magnificent, and so is she, so I will stand up for my dream! By my example, I will inspire others to stand for theirs too."

When you begin to paint your masterpiece, keep in mind that the finish always starts in the mind. As you take out the brushes and begin to paint the canvas, never worry about the process. If the FINISH is in your mind, those who are meant to be a part of your dream will be on their way. Just keep taking the hits with a smile on your face, stand back up, face the doubters, and reply "I LIKE IT. Let's do it again!"

Many women ask me how I attract people to my team. Most often, my reply is, "When you believe without a shadow of a doubt in where you are going, and you're willing to allow the dream you are creating to help others, they will follow you without hesitation." You see, it's like this: if you have to convince yourself about your beliefs, then it's impossible to help others. Your lack of belief in the dream will partner with their fears, keeping anything great from emerging from this combination. Because our motives must be PURE when building a team and pursuing a dream, we must continually ask ourselves this question: "Am I willing to go on the battlefield without retrieval, or will I quit at the first sign of adversity?" People want a WARRIOR to help them because a true warrior will never leave the team on the field. They will always finish what they begin.

Having confidence and zero hesitation is the other major key. Otherwise, the team you attract will lack the commitment to pursue the magnificent. Billy Graham once asked a little boy how to get to the post office in a town he was visiting. The little guy gladly gave him directions. Dr. Graham told the little boy that if he came to his meeting that night, he was going to tell everyone how to get to heaven. After thinking for a moment, the little boy looked at Billy Graham and said, "Oh, no sir, I won't be there. You don't even know how to get to the post office! How in the world can you teach me how to get to heaven?" The same is true in your journey. In order for the right people to gladly join your dream, you must know what your masterpiece looks like and where you are going.

When I bring leaders onto my team, they don't wonder if I am going to be around next week or ten years from now, and they are confident that I know exactly where we are going. They are 100% *positive* I will stand no matter what hits come my way. Forever. Quitters can only inspire others to quit. If you want to grow and see your team grow as well, then you must say goodbye to *doubt* and say hello to *fierce faith* in where you are going.

We don't just want any team, however; we desire CHAMPIONS. Michael Jordan once said, "Talent will win games; but teamwork and intelligence win championships." The team's success is ultimately in the leader's hands as you play like a champion and take a stand. Great warriors listen to the wisdom of those who have gone before them and choose to apply what they hear. Many people have good intentions, but they quit when it gets too hard. I have to say this because it is often said to me in my business: new recruits are *so* excited to pursue the magnificent, and they are absolutely SURE that this is what God wanted them to do. However, the minute it gets tough, they decide that it must not be God's will and quit. Seriously? That is the biggest LIE on the planet. You see, God doesn't change His mind—*we* do! Isn't it much more respectable to just own up to this rather than blame God?

Just like with everything else, we attract the team when we believe in the dream. I truly believe that planting seeds of joy, hope, faith, and love brings nothing but limitless possibilities in our future. It just requires a firm belief in the dream even in the absence of proof.

Champions never want to discuss a plan B. As they play with excellence, they expect to exceed the limits of what they thought they could achieve. I totally believe the scoreboard matters in pursuing the dream. It helps you pay attention to how well you are playing and helps continue to improve in the process of winning your championship. All great warriors play to WIN, as winning helps others be inspired too. John Maxwell once said, "There will be drop outs, you know the players that fail to take responsibility, the cop outs who are the players that make excuses for why they aren't responsible, hold outs are the players who waiver and long to take responsibility, and then there are ALL OUTS, the leaders who take ownership."

The all-outs own the responsibility and take action because they choose to stand. Success is planned, and great teams have every intention of making things happen. They don't wait for success to fall in their laps. Champions strive to set the standards and raise the bar so they are assured a victory. Winston Churchill said, "I have nothing to offer but blood, toil, tears and sweat ... You ask, what is our aim? I can answer in one word: It is victory, victory at all costs, victory in spite of all terror, victory, however long and hard the road may be; for without victory, there is no survival."

A warrior doesn't have to be talked into taking a stand; they have a passion to be the FIRST to stand and lead the way. It took some *serious* courage for me to pursue my masterpiece, and you know what? I am SO VERY GLAD I stood up. Dorothy Bernard said, "Courage is rightly esteemed the first of human qualities because it is the quality that guarantees all others. Courage is fear that has said its prayers." Courage begins within the heart and mind of every single great warrior that ever pursued their dream. Billy Graham described courage like this: "Courage is letting go of the familiar and forging ahead, it is contagious." He continued, "When a brave man takes a stand, the spines of others are stiffened."

The courage of a leader will inspire, and fear will only limit you. John Maxwell writes "How ironic that those who don't have the courage to take risks and those who do experience the same amount of fear in life." I often wonder how David in the Bible must have felt as a lowly shepherd boy when he faced Goliath. Goliath was a giant, and the greatest of armies ran and hid in fear when they faced Goliath—but not David. David ran to the challenge with ZERO HESITATION—just like my son Sam when he stepped out on the field knowing he would be hit by the stronger team. There was no fear in David because he already saw the victory in his mind. He took his stones and his slingshot and decided to STAND. We all know how that story ends—all because David stood with courage. A leader who makes the decision to stand will demonstrate this by commitment. In doing this, the universe shifts in our favor. The world is crying out for the warriors to get "SOULED" out and take a stand for something that is much greater than the tangible things in life. We must take a stand for LOVE, just like the gardener of the rich man did. Keeping a dream all to yourself is just selfish, as a masterpiece is meant to be shared with others.

A few years ago we were in Disney World around the New Year, and we were "standing" in line to go on the ride called Soarin'. We had been on this ride several times before, so we were considered pros. As we waited in line, there were three little children and their parents standing beside us, and I could sense that the parents were just not sure about this ride. They eventually asked me if their little ones would be okay riding it. I said, "Of course! It is *so* amazing! They will LOVE this ride!" I proceeded to explain to her that it will seem like they are going up really high, but it's exaggerated in their minds because of the special effects. I could almost feel their hesitation. You may know what that's like—you are afraid the people around you can feel your fear. Keep this in mind if you want to lead because fear is as contagious as faith; but it will deliver two profoundly different results.

The couple's oldest son Luke seemed super excited to go on the ride. In fact, you could feel his excitement because there was zero hesitation on his part. He just *knew* this was going to be the ride of his life. By the world's perspective, people might say that Luke was "challenged" because he was different from not only his brother and sister, but from many children his own age. But by God's standards, Luke was MAGNIFICENT. I believe that Luke understood courage because he came right up to me with zero hesitation, put his hand out boldly, and said, "Hi, my name is Luke." He proceeded to introduce us to his sister Sarah and his brother John. He assured everyone that he was not afraid.

My son Sam noticed that Luke was special and decided to connect with these children. He offered to sit by them and encourage them through this amazing experience. As we sat down on the ride and "soared" into the sky, Sarah, John, and Luke were beside us, side-by-side, taking a stand that we would experience this ride together. They knew it was going to be great because they TRUSTED us to coach them through the journey.

When the ride was over and we said our goodbyes to that family, Sammy looked at me and said, "Isn't that weird, Mom? You meet people for a moment, and then they are gone?"

I replied, "Yes, it is, Sam."

He proceeded to say, "But then you meet people that stay with you for a lifetime. Isn't that weird?"

"Yes, it is, Sam," I again replied. That day, I shared with Sam that I do not believe in coincidences. In fact, I believe that everything happens for a reason, and we have an opportunity every single day to make a difference in a person's life—whether for better or worse. When we encourage others, we lift them up to places where they can soar.

But when we instill fear and doubt in them, we can destroy any chance of their ability to experience the ride of their life and operate in magnificence. Luke demonstrated that he had the courage to reach out, connect, and trust us to lead them on the ride and showed that we could do it together. Luke took a stand by following something deep inside that gave him the faith to get on the ride. And guess what?! This inspired his entire family to experience the ride. Without Luke's stand and our encouragement, they may have allowed fear to prevent them from getting on. I believe if an innocent child can trust his heart enough to take a stand in order to soar, it is a great lesson to all of us that we can too. I believe that Luke took a stand to LOVE for a moment, and he touched my heart. I am positively sure that Luke has now inspired your life as well.

I treasure the opportunity every single day to stand so that I can continue to pursue the magnificent. My life has been forever changed because I picked up the brushes that were handed to me and just started to paint, day by day, with the colors of my dream. Pursuing our dream ignites the fire in ourselves and in those around us, leaving a legacy.

The multiplication factor of leadership is vision, faith, courage, passion, and love. LOVE is a legacy worth more than all the gold in the world. After all, the greatest gift in heaven and earth is love. Love has transformed my life, and my hope is that you will open your heart to your masterpiece of magnificence, the people you have not yet met, and the love that will grow in abundance because one warrior is willing to get on the field take the hits and continue to STAND. The hits will inspire you even more to live your dream with intense passion and stand for those who may be hesitating to get on the field—but they are waiting for YOU to pass the belief on to them.

Kent M. Keith wrote the following, and they were found on Mother Theresa's walls. He said, "When people are illogical, unreasonable, and self-centered, love them anyway. If you do good, people will accuse you of selfish motives; but do good anyway. If you are successful, you will win false friends and true enemies; but succeed anyway. The biggest men and women with the biggest ideas can be shot down by the smallest men and women with the smallest minds but THINK BIG anyway. People favor underdogs but follow only TOP DOGS. Fight for a few underdogs anyway. What you spend years building may be destroyed overnight but build anyway. People really need help but may attack you if you do help them but help people anyway. Give the world the best you have, and you will get knocked in the teeth; but give the world the best you have anyway."

If you really are a warrior, then it's time to get out on the field of dreams, take the hits, STAND, and reply, "I LIKE IT. Let's do it again!"

YOUR CHOICE, YOUR LIFE, YOUR MASTERPIECE.